MORE
FRONT-LINE
ESSEX

MORE
FRONT-LINE
ESSEX

MICHAEL FOLEY

THE HISTORY PRESS

First published in the United Kingdom in 2008 by
The History Press
The Mill · Brimscombe Port · Stroud · Gloucestershire · GL5 2QG

British Library Cataloguing in Publication Data
A catalogue record for this book is available from the British Library.

ISBN 978-0-7509-4951-4

To Tyler, Rebecca, Kyra, Tommy and Olivia

Typeset in 10.5/13pt Galliard.
Typesetting and origination by
The History Press.
Printed and bound in England.

Contents

Introduction

Since completing *Front-Line Essex* in 2005, I have continued to research the military background of the county. I quickly realised that there were not only many areas that I had not covered in my first book, but that I had also missed out much of what happened in the areas that I did cover, although each town, barracks and camp in the history of Essex could of course provide enough material for a book of their own. Some have already had one written, but unfortunately most of these books relating to military history are very difficult to come by. Hopefully, then, *More Front-Line Essex* will fill some gaps in the knowledge of its readers and also allow everyone to see some of the fine old pictures that I have managed to obtain, and which may otherwise have disappeared into private collections never to be seen by anyone but their owners.

Michael Foley
www.authorsites.co.uk/michaelfoley

Acknowledgements

The author would like to express his thanks to the following people for permission to use their photographs: John Smith and Nick Challoner of www.challoner.com//aviation and the Ford Motor Company.

All other illustrations are from the author's private collection. Although every attempt has been made to find the copyright owners of all the illustrations, anyone whose copyright has been unintentionally breached should contact the author through the publisher.

ONE

Pre-Norman Conquest Essex

Essex has been the scene of conflict between its inhabitants and invaders from overseas from the earliest days of its history. The Trinovantes tribe controlled much of the county for centuries until much fiercer tribes from the continent began to arrive shortly before the first Roman conquest. The Belgic tribes pushed the Trinovantes further inland, a process that continued, apart from a brief period of respite after Caesar forced them to desist.

It was during the later Claudian invasion that the Romans finally defeated the Belgae and took their capital at Camulodunum. Apart from the very short spell of Iceni rule in Essex, the Romans continued to govern the county until they left in about the fourth century.

Information on the years between the departure of the Romans and the new invaders from Scandinavia are less easy to discover. The Saxons no doubt arrived and settled in the county, and must have come into conflict with the present inhabitants

The Iceni – who sacked Colchester and slaughtered the Roman inhabitants – from the Colchester Pageant of 1909.

of the period. The Saxons did not come as a mass invasion, as did the Romans, but arrived in smaller groups and separate tribes who then settled in different areas. It was only later, in the Saxon period, that written records appeared and by then the Vikings had began to make their presence felt.

Raids by the Norsemen later became invasions, until Essex became part of Danelaw in the ninth century. Although King Alfred often fought the Danes successfully, it was his descendants who finally drove them out. This was far from the end however, and Essex was the scene of further battles between Saxons and Danes until the eleventh century, when England came under the control of a Danish king. The return of the Saxons in the shape of Edward the Confessor and then Harold was very short lived and ended with the arrival of William.

BRADWELL

Bradwell was the site of one of the Roman forts of the Saxon Shore. The common view of these defences is that they were built as a defence against Saxon Raiders towards the end of the Roman period in Britain. There is sometimes another view put forward that the forts were built by Carausius, who had declared himself Emperor of Britain, and that the forts were a defence against an attack by soldiers of the Empire trying to reclaim Britain. Both points of view could have a level of truth in that some of the supposed forts of the Saxon Shore date from a much earlier period. It may even be that, after the death of the usurper Carausius, the forts were used as defences against the Saxons.

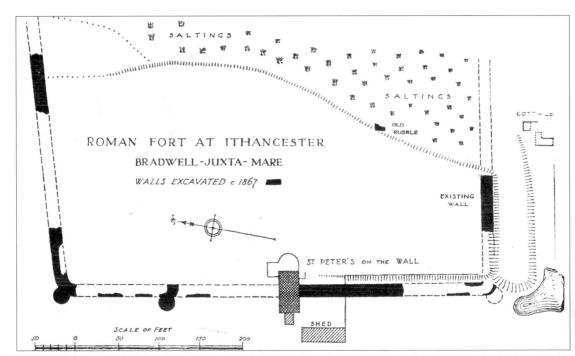

The Roman fort at Bradwell. It is believed that the Church of St Peter on the Wall may be built over the fort's entrance.

The fort at Bradwell is believed to have been the one known as Othona. In the fourth century it was manned by a force of men from the North African part of the Empire. The fort was square with 12ft thick walls and a bastion at one corner. It is thought to have been around six acres in size but the sea has long ago washed part of this area away.

The fort was excavated in the mid-nineteenth century but no gateway was found, and it is thought that the chapel of St Peter may have been built over the fort's entrance in the seventh century using building material from the defences. The fort would no doubt have already been in ruins by the time the church was built.

There have been reports of the foundations of several Roman buildings being found under the ground and it seems there may have been a larger settlement alongside the fort. This was often the case with Roman forts where settlements grew around them to provide services to the men of the garrison.

COLCHESTER

Colchester was already an important settlement and fortress before the Romans arrived. It was originally the home of members of the Trinovantes. The tribe were being harried by the Belgae invaders from the continent and were actually saved by the first Roman invasion led by Julius Caesar. He forced the Belgae to leave the Trinovantes alone. After Caesar returned to Gaul however, the Belgae began their attempts at conquest again and drove the Trinovantes further inland.

Camulodunum then became the Belgae capital. When the Romans again came under the command of Aulus Plautius, they defeated the Britons and the Emperor

The Balkerne Gate at Colchester: part of the Roman wall that surrounded the town.

Claudius himself led the march into Camulodunum. The battle for the town supposedly included the use of elephants by the Romans.

The town later became the site of a Roman retirement base for ex-legionnaires. It was to this town that the Iceni came. They destroyed it and slaughtered its inhabitants before moving on to London. The town was later refortified with stronger walls. There was an increase in the Roman presence in East Anglia after the Iceni uprising, which included the building of a number of forts. Most did not last as long as Colchester.

When the Romans left Britain the town was still occupied. The early Saxon invaders supposedly had little love for towns, but as they took over, the area surrounding it must have eventually become occupied by them. The common view is that the previous occupants of the area were forced to move inland and eventually the original Britons occupied the western side of the country, but there is no clear evidence as to when Colchester became a Saxon town or whether they originally mixed with its established residents.

By the tenth century, the Danes controlled Colchester until Edward the Elder led the local population against the town and drove them out. Those Danes left in the town were supposedly slaughtered.

MALDON

When Alfred the Great died in 899 most of Essex was still under the control of the Vikings. Alfred's son, Edward, camped at Maldon with his army while he inspected defences that had been built in Witham. In 916 Edward also built defences at

The Vikings were constant visitors to the Essex coast and fought a victorious battle at Maldon.

Maldon, which were part of a series of forts in the country. In 917 Edward defeated the Danes at Colchester but was then himself attacked at Maldon. Although this attack was driven off it was not to be the last Viking attack on the town.

When Ethelred the Unready came to the throne in 991, a large Viking fleet raiding along the east coast came to Maldon, no doubt attracted by the mint, which had been set up by Athelstan. They took Northey Island. A well-known earldorman at that time, Brihtnoth, who owned a number of estates in Essex and was renowned for protecting the monasteries, led an army against them.

Brihtnoth took up his position by the ford from Northey Island. It seems that the Saxon leader was unusually chivalrous in what would have been a less than honourable time and allowed the Vikings to cross to the mainland to fight the battle. This led to the death of the Saxon leader and the retreat of his men.

MERSEA ISLAND

After capturing Colchester, the Romans used Mersea Island to lay up their boats for the winter. Some villas were built on the island, but the most amazing site from the period is the Mersea Island Barrow or Mount.

The Romans did not build barrows and it was thought that the barrow might have been the burial place of an important Briton, as only the most distinguished people were buried in such large erections. It is possible that the occupant may have been a hostage taken after the Romans defeated Caractacus, son of Cunobelin, during the Claudian invasion. Alternatively, it may have even been one of his sons.

The cremated remains of the body in the barrow were put in a Roman green glass bowl and then placed in a lead box. The jar is now in Colchester Museum. This would seem to point to the remains being of a person honoured by the Romans, or perhaps the deceased was indeed a Roman. In the eighteenth-century *History of Essex* by Holman there is a reference to a second barrow on the island.

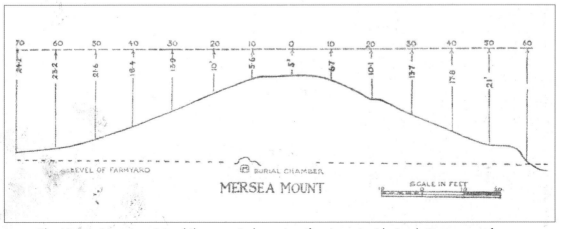

The Mersea Mount contained the cremated remains of an important but unknown person from the Roman period.

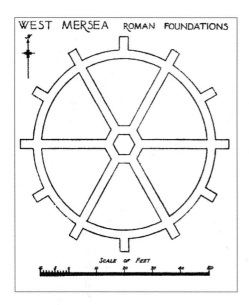

WEST MERSEA   ROMAN FOUNDATIONS

SCALE OF FEET

The remains of an unusual round Roman building was also found close to West Mersea church. The foundations were discovered while digging a sawpit in 1896. The walls were 3ft thick and had a number of buttresses for columns both inside and outside the walls. There is no definite proof of what the building was, but it could have been a lighthouse or a watchtower.

The unusual foundations of a Roman building found on Mersea Island. It could have been a watchtower or lighthouse.

MUCKING

The area of Mucking began to arouse interest in the 1960s when crop marks showed what was thought to be a the remains of a Neolithic henge. It eventually turned out to be a Bronze Age earthwork. Further investigation has shown that Mucking was a settlement that dated from prehistoric times up until the Anglo-Saxon period.

The earthwork was described as a mini hill fort, the position of which would have been ideal for controlling travel along the River Thames. There was also an Iron Age fort or enclosure built overlooking Mucking Creek.

The area also displayed evidence of Roman occupation, but this was mainly of an agricultural type, so it seems that the strategic position of the earlier times were not as important to the Romans. Perhaps this was because they were more secure in their ownership of the whole country. This seems to have also been the case with later Saxon habitation, which was mainly based on agriculture.

UPHALL CAMP

Alongside the River Roding at Ilford is the site of an extensive Iron Age camp. It has been estimated as once having covered nearly fifty acres. There was also a large mound included within the camp, which had disappeared by the late nineteenth century.

The area was described as an Iron Age fortified settlement in a report by English Heritage. There was only limited evidence of Bronze Age and Roman occupation. It is thought that the defence could have been a Trinovantian stronghold. Whether this was originally on the edge of their lands or was occupied after the tribe were driven inland by the Belgic tribes who invaded their lands nearer the coast is not known.

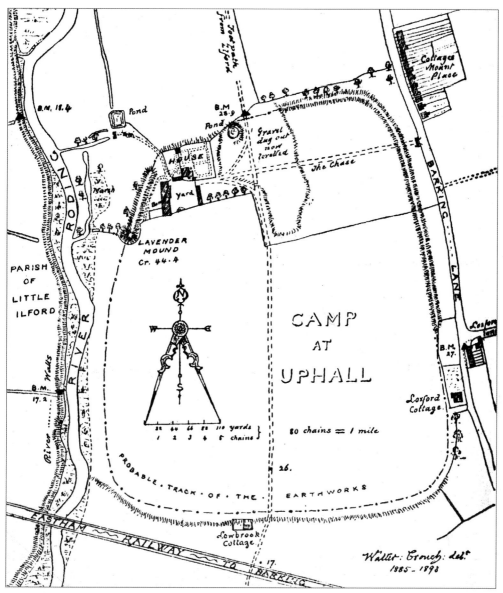

Uphall Camp was an Iron Age fort, which may have also been used by the Romans, the Vikings and the Normans.

Very close to the site was a brickfield, which, during the nineteenth century, became a well-known site for finding the bones of several ancient animals such as mammoth and rhinoceros. One complete mammoth skull from the site is now in the Natural History Museum.

Evidence of Iron Age workings have been found on the Uphall site and so it seems that the camp predated the Romans, although it is believed that the Romans later used it, which led one historian named Lieheuillier in 1750 to argue that the site was too large for a camp and was in fact a Roman town. He argued that building materials from the town were taken to repair nearby Barking Abbey after the Danes burnt it down.

There have been several Roman finds on the site and no doubt it would have been an ideal spot for Roman ships coming up the Thames and into the Roding, but representing it as a town may be taking the description too far.

When the Danes destroyed Barking Abbey in 870, much of the local area was under Danish control. Once again it has been argued that Uphall was probably a Danish stronghold and for some time it was believed that this was in fact its origin. Lieutenant General Pitt Rivers – the Inspector General of Ancient Monuments in the late nineteenth century – was a strong believer in this view.

It is also thought that after the Norman Conquest, when William was staying at Barking Abbey while the Tower of London was built, Uphall was used as a base for his troops.

I have never heard of any proof being found of Viking or Norman occupation, but it would be quite believable that such a well constructed and strategically placed defensive position would have been used by any forces that were in the area for any length of time.

TWO

From the Norman Conquest to Napoleon

Although Essex may not have been the site of a battle related to the Norman invasion, it was not long after the Battle of Hastings that William arrived in the county. The new king actually lived at Barking Abbey while his new castle, the Tower of London, was built further along the River Thames.

In later years, King John was busy in the county during the dispute with the rebel Barons and their ally the Dauphin of France. Essex was the gathering point of later armies when Elizabeth I visited her men ready to fight the Armada at Tilbury.

Ongar Castle was originally a Norman motte and bailey castle built by Richard de Lucy. It was demolished in the sixteenth century and replaced with a brick building.

Colchester Castle was one of the largest Norman castles in England.

Saffron Walden Castle was built in the early twelfth century but was destroyed by Henry II shortly after. Rebuilt in the fourteenth century, it was mostly demolished in the eighteenth century.

When a long battle was later fought in Essex the enemy was from within. The siege of Colchester took place with both sides being English during the Civil War. The later Dutch Wars took place in Kent and Suffolk and mostly missed Essex, with the exception of some stolen sheep on Canvey Island and the legend of the church tower at Coalhouse Fort being destroyed by cannon fire from their ships.

COALHOUSE FORT

It is believed that Henry VIII's blockhouse in East Tilbury had been built on a chantry site. Some of the stone used may have come from nearby St Margaret's Chapel. It was developed at a later date, but had a much more chequered career than nearby Tilbury Fort. The original defence was built at Coalhouse Point and contained fifteen cannon. Although the armaments were increased a few years later, the blockhouse then fell into disuse. Part of the sea wall was removed which led to flooding. The site of the original blockhouse was roughly half a mile south of Coalhouse Fort.

When the Earl of Leicester gathered his army at West Tilbury to fight the Armada, he showed some concern over nearby Tilbury Fort but had little interest in the blockhouse at East Tilbury. It would seem that the site was still derelict when the Dutch attacked the area and supposedly damaged the church tower, which was very close to the blockhouse. Although the common belief is that Dutch fire damaged the tower, there are opposing views about who was responsible, and it is possible that the missiles may have come from English ships. Another version of the incident includes a vicarage that was also destroyed by cannon fire.

It was to be another forty years before the battery was re-armed with more and larger guns. Then the battery was turned into a fort. It consisted of a semicircular defence facing the river, with a 60ft moat surrounding the whole structure.

COLCHESTER

The Norman Conquest led to one large change in the town of Colchester. It was essentially still a walled town, as it had been since Roman times, but the Normans added something new, the castle. What remains today may look impressive, but at the time it was built the castle was just the central building in a much larger complex. This included a series of earthworks around the central tower. The Norman lord of the castle and town was Eudo Dapifer.

Colchester Castle was once part of a much larger complex surrounded by a large series of earthworks.

The Ramparts were an ancient defensive position used by Fairfax and his men during the siege of Colchester in the Civil War.

Eudo was quite popular with the inhabitants and founded St John's Abbey. The town prospered under their lord and it grew outside of the town walls. Colchester managed to avoid any serious inclusion in the numerous uprisings and conflicts between the lords and the kings in the following years. This was more than made up for by the siege during the Civil War.

On 12 June 1648, a Royalist army numbering around 3,000 men arrived at Colchester from Kent. The original plan seemed to be for them to rest in the town for a short time, but the arrival of Parliamentary forces put a stop to this and led to the siege. Fairfax's Parliamentary army was camped at Lexden on the site of an ancient entrenchment known as the Ramparts.

The siege lasted twelve weeks, during which time the city walls were battered by artillery fire. It was to be starvation that led to the town's final surrender. The Royalist rank and file were let off lightly, and only a few of the Royalist leaders – including Lucas and Lisle – were executed after the surrender. Lucas had been one of the best cavalry commanders of the Royalist forces, which would have been good enough reason for his death. However, there is evidence that after being captured by the Parliamentary forces in 1646, Lucas received parole by promising not to fight them again. The pair were also described as mere soldiers of fortune, which was perhaps another reason for their deaths.

The inhabitants of the town seemed to have suffered greater hardship than the Royalist soldiers, especially unfair considering they had little option about being involved in the siege. More than 200 houses had been destroyed during the conflict, after which the townsfolk were fined £14,000 and forced to pay to have the town's walls demolished.

The siege house still bears marks of gunfire from the time of the Civil War siege of the town.

HADLEIGH

Hadleigh Castle was built in 1231 as the guard post over the entrance to the Thames and the route into London. The castle once boasted seven towers and 8ft-thick walls. It was often occupied by the kings of the land, and in particular by Edward I, II and III. While they were in residence, jousting tournaments were held on the green. Henry VIII gave the castle as a gift to three of his wives.

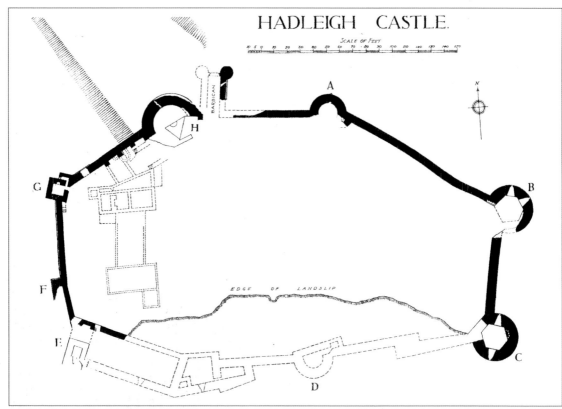

Hadleigh Castle once had seven towers. The broken lines show where part of the castle collapsed owing to a landslip.

An early nineteenth-century print of Hadleigh Castle, showing that it was already in ruins at this time.

The defences often overlooked the assembly of English fleets. The fleet that went to fight the Armada sailed from the river close to the castle, and the fleet that later went to fight the Dutch left from the then large naval port of nearby Leigh. In medieval times the area was a well-known shipbuilding centre.

During the sixteenth and seventeenth centuries, a number of famous naval men came from the town of Leigh. The Haddocks were one of the best-known Leigh families. Admiral Sir Richard Haddock was involved in the Dutch Wars of the seventeenth century, and took part in the Battle of Southwold Bay off the Suffolk coast. Sir Richard's son, Nicholas Haddock, also became an admiral. As well as the two admirals, there were also seven naval captains in the family. Another local family with strong connections with the sea were the Salmons. Robert Salmon, who died in 1591, was the Master of Trinity House, while Peter Salmon was doctor to Charles I.

Part of the remains of Hadleigh Castle, showing the south-east tower.

Leigh, close to the site of Hadleigh Castle, and was once a major shipbuilding area.

HARWICH

By the middle of the sixteenth century, walls enclosed much of the town of Harwich. There were also a number of towers incorporated into the walls; these were mainly facing the sea. These defences were further increased at the same time that the blockhouses were being built at Tilbury by Henry VIII. There were in fact three bulwarks at Harwich in 1551: at Middle House, House on the Hill (later the site of the Redoubt) and Tower House. There were also two blockhouses at Landguard Point and Landguard Road. Queen Elizabeth I visited the town to inspect the defences in 1561. The defences did not have a large permanent force in occupation during peacetime, only a captain, a lieutenant and a porter. During times of crisis there would also be a regular garrison. By 1588 there were forty-six guns mounted in the town's defences.

Because of the town's strategic importance and because news from Europe reached Harwich before anywhere else in the country, the road to London was vital. Parliament changed responsibility for road maintenance from the parish system for the first time in 1695 to give care of the London–Harwich road to the Quarter Sessions. Turnpikes did not raise enough money to keep the road in good order, so a rate was levied on all roadside parishes from Brentwood to the coast.

History and Traditions
of
The Essex Regiment

44TH. PERIOD 1768

56TH, PERIOD 1792

The Essex Regiment was created from the 44th and 56th Regiments of Foot. They served in Essex and around the world.

HEDINGHAM

The castle at Hedingham was built around 1140 and overlooks the Colne Valley from the top of a hill. For most of its early history it was owned by the de Vere family. Aubrey or Alberic de Vere built the castle after his father came to Britain with William the Conqueror. It was built during the civil war in the reign of King Stephen. When the castle's builder died, it passed to his son of the same name. The defences have been added to over the years and the walls are now nearly 100ft high and 12ft thick.

The castle saw action when it was besieged by the followers of King John, but was later handed over to Louis, the Dauphin of France, who had come to England to support the rebel lords who were against John. The de Vere family finally got the castle back and became the Earls of Oxford, a title they kept for many years.

Several changes were made to the castle during the Dutch Wars of the seventeenth century to deter the authorities from allowing the castle to be used as a prison for Dutch prisoners or as a billet for soldiers.

Castle Hedingham was built by the de Vere family, who owned it for much of its life.

Castle Hedingham was besieged by King John in 1216 during his dispute with the rebel barons supported by the Dauphin of France.

John Hawkwood was the second son of a tanner of Sible Hedingham in the fourteenth century, and was a member of a company of soldiers raised by John de Vere of Hedingham who went to fight for Edward III in France. There is a story that John was knighted on the field of battle after impressing the Black Prince with his skills.

After the end of the war with France, John Hawkwood joined other ex-members of the English army in becoming mercenaries and enlisted with the Marquis of Monferrat, an Italian ruler, to help him fight the rulers of Milan. Hawkwood supposedly became the leader of a mercenary group who were responsible for burning more than fifty towns and villages. Hawkwood then took his company to fight in the war between Pisa and Florence. In fact, during his time in the country, Hawkwood fought for many of the small Italian states, often becoming an ally of his previous enemies.

Hawkwood ended his days in Florence and his fame in the country led to his being given a large funeral on his

Not all reports of John Hawkwood were noble. The peace of 1360 found him short of money so he led a band of men who spent their time plundering in France.

death in 1394. There seems to be a mystery surrounding the position of his remains. Richard II supposedly requested of Florence that his body be allowed to be brought home. There seems to be no evidence that this happened. There was however either a tomb or a memorial to Hawkwood in the church in Sible Hedingham. Despite much argument as to whether his body was actually there, it is now thought that it is.

Hawkwood's son, John, from his first marriage, returned to Sible Hedingham and was knighted early in the fifteenth century. John's sister supposedly married Sir William Coggeshall, so despite the possibility of their father's remains still being in Italy, the family kept its Essex connections.

MALDON

In 1628 Maldon was graced by the presence of some Irish soldiers who were billeted in the town. It seems that the soldiers were not as respectable or orderly as one would expect them to be. Locals petitioned the authorities for their removal, claiming that they were no longer masters in their own homes and needed to guard their property while being under the constant threat of violence.

The situation came to a head on St Patrick's Day when a riot broke out in the town. Over thirty townsmen were wounded and several of the soldiers were shot. The soldiers were then moved to Witham.

As well as its life as a port, Maldon also had a hand in providing ships for the navy. In 1654, the frigate *Jersey* was built in the town. For a time its captain was the famous diarist Samuel Pepys.

MERSEA ISLAND

Mersea Island was once the site of an old fort, probably built during the reign of Henry VIII during the war with France. It was quite large; the sides were 300ft in length with turrets at each corner, and had gun platforms along its sides. It was also surrounded by a defensive moat.

After the war, in 1551, the guns were removed but it seems that the fort was still garrisoned in 1558. By the end of the century the building had fallen into disrepair. A Royalist force occupied it during the siege of Colchester until Parliamentary Dragoons captured it on 14 June 1648. Troops from the fort were used to reinforce the crews of ships that intercepted Royalist frigates trying to reach besieged Colchester by sailing up the River Colne. This took place a few days after the Parliamentary forces took the defences and seems to have been the final conflict that occurred at the fort. There were troops posted there during the later Dutch Wars but by the early eighteenth century the fort seemed to have disappeared.

PLESHEY

Pleshey Castle was an original Norman wooden motte and bailey defence with extensive outer walls surrounding the town. It was built in the eleventh century by Geoffrey De Manville, one of William's commanders at Hastings. The castle had a moat surrounding it. Although supposedly dismantled in the mid-twelfth century,

The bridge across the moat at Pleshey Castle is thought to date from the fifteenth century.

the castle was rebuilt at the end of the century in stone. Much of the castle was destroyed in the seventeenth century when the stones were used for building material.

Geoffrey De Manville died around 1100. His son, William, died in 1129 and was succeeded by his grandson, another Geoffrey, who became the Earl of Essex under King Stephen. He was to die fighting in one of the numerous rebellions of the time and his son, also Geoffrey, became the earl under Henry II. Shortly afterwards the wooden Pleshey Castle was demolished, but after Geoffrey's death his brother William rebuilt the castle in stone.

The castle later became the property of the 1st Earl of Hereford, Henry de Bohun, whose wife was the daughter of Edward I. The castle later passed into the hands of the Duke of Gloucester, Thomas of Woodstock, son of Edward III, who was exiled from Pleshey to France by Richard II in 1397 and was later murdered in Calais. Another duke who opposed the king was the Duke of Exeter, who was executed at Pleshey by Richard shortly after his uncle died. The castle is mentioned in Shakespeare's *Richard II*.

There is little left of the castle today apart from the earthworks and a bridge across the moat, thought to date from the fifteenth century.

RAYLEIGH

Rayleigh was the site of a motte and bailey castle probably built around the end of the eleventh century. The castle was mentioned in the Domesday Book of 1086 and was therefore one of the first Norman castles in the country. It was built by Sweyne of Essex, the son of Robert FitzWimarc.

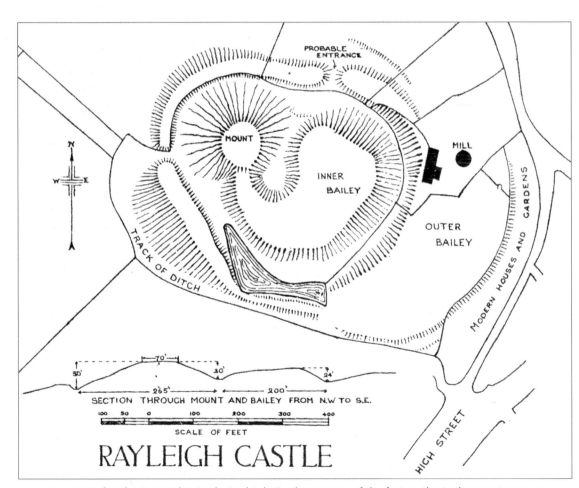

Mentioned in the Domesday Book, Rayleigh Castle was one of the first castles in the country.

It was not in use for long, as in 1163 the castle and land fell into the hands of Henry of Essex who was defeated in a trial by combat by Simon de Montfort after being accused of cowardice. The land and castle reverted to the crown and by the fourteenth century the castle was in ruins.

There are no remains above ground but a great deal of stone and rubble was found during excavations in the early twentieth century. The castle was in a strong position overlooking the Crouch Valley. Houses have now been built on the castle mound.

TILBURY FORT

It is thought that West Tilbury was once a Roman settlement and was one of their crossing points of the Thames. Indeed, it continues to be a ferry site today. It is also believed to have been the site of a monastery founded by St Cedd in his attempts to convert the Saxons. West Tilbury was still no more than a small village when it had its first connections with the military. The building of the original fort probably did not have much effect on the village, as it is quite some distance away, built in a marshy area on the bank of the Thames. The village did not change very much until the end of the nineteenth century when the docks were built. According to some, even the coming of the docks did not change the area greatly.

West Tilbury had been the site of an ancient medieval hospital. Many of the hospitals in the country changed from treating the sick to becoming almshouses, chantry chapels or even hermitages due to lack of funds. The blockhouse built in West Tilbury was known as the Hermitage blockhouse so this could have been the site's original purpose. As Henry VIII seized many chantries when he took over church lands, it seems he may have saved money by using these confiscated lands as sites for his blockhouses.

The reign of Elizabeth I was no more settled than her father's when it came to threats from Europe. In 1588 a camp for troops was created in West Tilbury in response to the threat of the Spanish Armada. The menace of Spanish invasion had been hanging over the country for years. Three years prior to the Tilbury Camp's conception, the Spanish had landed and burnt the small town of Mousehole in Cornwall. The ease with which they did it and the lack of opposition had led to calls to improve defences around the coast.

The Lieutenant General for the Defence of the Realm, the Earl of Leicester, commanded the Tilbury Camp. Leicester visited the Tilbury Fort on a number of occasions and remarked on its poor state of repair. He asked for more powder for the guns to be delivered. Firing of the guns at the fort upon an enemy was to be a signal for local men to rush to help fight the invader. It was not only gunpowder that was in short supply. Proclamations had been read out in local market towns asking for food suppliers to come to Tilbury. It seems however that very few appeared.

The camp for Leicester's troops was some distance from the fort, nearer the village. There were ten regiments stationed at the camp; two of these were from Essex. They had been the first footmen to arrive although some cavalry had preceded them.

Queen Elizabeth I visited the camp at Tilbury at the time of the Armada to rally the troops.

Although Tilbury Fort commands a strong defensive position on the Thames, it was left to decline until it became almost useless.

Queen Elizabeth I wished to visit the camps that were built for her troops and, although Leicester thought that camps near the coast were too dangerous for her, he agreed to let her come to Tilbury. His idea was that Elizabeth would stay at her palace at Havering, which was only fourteen miles away. Leicester also wanted her to have a guard of 2,000 men stationed at Romford.

Elizabeth stayed near Tilbury, probably not at Havering, but by the time she reached the camp the Armada had already been dispersed. The army was disbanded in August, but a large number of the Essex men marched to Harwich where they stayed for another month.

The presence of the camp was not without problems for the local population. The church close to the camp reported that the wall had been broken down and stools needed repair. It seems that the bricks from the wall made good stoves for cooking while the stools made good firewood. Many of the local churchwardens also had to be replaced as they had left to go and serve in the army. One of the strangest events connected to the camp occurred at Colchester. Thomas Cockerell was about to be married when the captain to whom he was attached arrived and took him away to Tilbury.

The fort, although upgraded, was not kept in a very high standard of repair throughout the sixteenth century. During the seventeenth century there were problems with farm animals wandering into the fort from the fields, or which had come off the ferry and into the enclosure. The ferry house was inside the fort itself, so that any travellers had access to the guns.

? 40 miles

Unlike nearby Colchester, Tilbury played little part in the Civil War apart from use as a crossing point for Fairfax and his army. Captain Willoughby, a staunch Parliamentarian, was in command of the fort. His orders were to arrest all suspicious persons passing in ships upon the Thames.

A number of the Royalist prisoners from the siege at Colchester were later sent to Tilbury. These were followed by twenty Scotsmen, who were suspected of being officers of the Scottish army impersonating travellers.

Under Cromwell, the garrison was raised from twenty to sixty-four men. The buildings however continued to decline until Charles II came to the throne. He wanted to reorganise the country's defences, again in response to threats from Europe, and plans were drawn up in 1662 to strengthen the old fort at Tilbury. The plans were not however acted upon and in 1667, when the Dutch sailed up the Thames, the fort was in no condition to do anything about the attack.

The Duke of Albemarle came to Tilbury during the Dutch attack and found only two guns mounted. Samuel Pepys also arrived and claimed the fort would not have lasted half an hour if the Dutch had come further up river.

After going ashore on Canvey Island to steal food, the Dutch sailed up the Thames and fired on East Tilbury church. Work began on strengthening the Tilbury Fort soon after. Eighty guns were mounted between Tilbury and Gravesend. Workers were gathered from all over Essex to complete the defences and the king visited in 1671 to see how the work was progressing. It was however a slow process and it was 1680 before Tilbury was fully armed, but the work was still not complete and it took a further twelve years to finally complete the fort's defences.

The old ferry house had to be demolished when the fort was built, along with many other houses. It seems that a small community had grown around the fort and ferry house. It is believed by some that a tile factory owned by Daniel Defoe was also situated near the fort, but the exact site is unknown. The ferry house itself was moved to the site now occupied by the World's End public house, which was originally built as the new ferry house. A weekly cattle market was held at the World's End; many of the beasts for sale came across from Kent on the ferry.

The fort was designed by Sir Bernard de Gomme, who was General of Ordnance to Charles II. It was built to withstand an attack by artillery and had large earth embankments held in place by bricks. This was a defensive method of taking the pounding of artillery on the earthen walls. There were also moats to defend it from attack on land. The moats were controlled by sluices and could be emptied in freezing weather: a frozen moat was next to useless in stopping an attacking force.

Ten years after the fort was completed it was involved in its first action when it was attacked in the late 1690s, not by a foreign enemy but by an estimated force of 400 (some reports say 700) Irish mercenaries fighting for James II.

In the middle of the eighteenth century, the fort was used as a prison for Scottish Jacobites captured at the Battle of Culloden. They were brought up the Thames and were at first held on the ships that carried them and guarded by soldiers from Tilbury Fort. When disease broke out on board they were taken ashore and held in the powder magazine. The prisoners became a tourist attraction and visitors were charged sixpence by the fort's garrison to see them.

Tilbury was part of a river defence system that included another fort across the river at Gravesend. The location of the forts was planned so that they could fire on enemy ships while they were manoeuvring for tacking in the winding river. In comparison to the site of the Kent fort, Tilbury was very isolated. There was no decent water supply and the fort's inhabitants depended on rainwater for their supply. The officers therefore preferred to spend their time away from the Essex bank of the Thames and spent most of their time in Kent.

The ferry between the two forts was always an important part of the defences. During an exercise in the late eighteenth century, between 5,000 and 7,000 troops were carried across the river and back again in less than twelve hours.

WARLEY

By the time of the English Civil War, methods of fighting had changed. Where previously the armourer had been the main provider of fighting materials, it was now the gunsmith. To combat this threat to their trade, armourers would often advertise their wares as musket- or pistol-proof.

Warley was the site of a summer camp for the militia, and popular with sightseers for many years until permanent barracks were finally built there.

There was a change however in the type of armour worn. Instead of full suits of armour the civil war period led to the return of short breastplates. Laminated thighplates protected the upper legs and led to the nickname Lobsters being applied to those who wore them.

The effigy of Sir Denner Strut in Little Warley church shows the style of armour of the day. Strut was a Royalist and was in Colchester in 1648 until taken prisoner on the town's surrender. He survived the event but lost his estates and was fined £1,350.

THREE

The Napoleonic Period to the Twentieth Century

The French wars of the late eighteenth century led to an upsurge in military building to counter the threat of a French invasion. Although Essex had been the site of large temporary military camps for many years, barracks were rare before Napoleon came to power to threaten our shores. Some of the earliest barracks were built for cavalry and were sited at regular intervals around the borders of the county. These were followed by large camps at strategic defensive locations, including Warley, Colchester and Weeley, while Martello towers sprang up at vulnerable coastal points, often in the unhealthy marshy areas of the coast.

Many of the Martello towers built during the Napoleonic Wars still survive. The tower at West Parade in Clacton was at one time used by the coastguard.

One of the Clacton towers near St Osyth has been renovated and is now used as an arts centre.

BOW

During the nineteenth century much of what is now East London was still part of Essex. The ancient site of West Ham Abbey played a big part in the development of a new form of weapon that had helped to defeat the French at Waterloo.

Rockets as weapons were first experienced by the British when fighting in India. Arthur Wellesley, later to become the Duke of Wellington, was not impressed by them – an opinion that he was to harbour for some time.

One man who was impressed was William Congrieve, the eldest son of an official at the Royal Laboratory at Woolwich. Congrieve invented warheads for rockets, which, although not very accurate, were much easier to transport than large artillery guns. The rockets were first used by the British in Boulogne Harbour in 1806 with some success. They were also used at the Battle of Waterloo in 1815 despite Wellington's dislike of them.

Congrieve later opened a factory in 1821 on the old Abbey site at Bow to make his rockets. The factory covered fourteen acres and was close to Three Mills, which had once included a gunpowder mill. Although the rockets were made at the factory, the Royal Gunpowder Mills at Waltham Abbey supplied the propellant used in the weapons.

After the factory closed in 1866, the site became a gasworks. Congrieve's name was to have a lingering connection with the area. When John Walker invented the friction match in 1830, he called them Congrieves after the rockets. The area around Bow and Stratford later became the site of numerous match factories, although the name of Congrieves was later dropped.

CHELMSFORD

At the early stages of the French wars the army were welcome visitors in Chelmsford and added some colour to what was at the time was a drab life for many inhabitants. Some of the military groups that travelled through the town also had bands accompanying them, which gave the whole area a carnival atmosphere.

There were rumours that plans had been made ready at the time of the outbreak of war to move the government to Chelmsford if the threatened invasion came. The threats were seen as more than just that. At the end of the eighteenth century there had already been an attempted landing by the French at Bantry Bay in Ireland – it was only foiled by bad weather.

This attempt was followed a few years later by a successful, if badly organised, landing by French forces near Fishguard in Wales. For a few days the French troops plundered local farms before surrendering to a mixed force of militiamen. The fact that the landing had been accomplished so easily did not give the country confidence in its coastal defences.

During the war there was a bewildering military merry-go-round of regiments that moved from one Essex barracks to another, including Chelmsford. Local newspapers would often list which regiment had moved from where and gave their destination. French spies would have had little more to do than buy a newspaper. Some regiments waited at Chelmsford to be made up to strength and then went abroad. Despite the new barracks in the town there were still men from the summer camps billeted in the homes of locals during the winter when they could not all fit into the barracks.

Probably the biggest expansion in any business in Chelmsford at the time was in the building trade. Not only were there barracks to be built but houses were needed for the increased population. The building of the barracks themselves employed over a hundred men. Alexander Copland had his own companies supplying building materials such as bricks and timber. Because of this he was able to build the barracks within a number of weeks.

There were also commercial buildings needed close to the river once the new canal linked the Chelmer to the Blackwater. The increase in building also led to expansion in support industries, such as brick making. And of course as the population grew so did the number of shops and inns. By the time the barracks opened there were over thirty shops in the town.

The arrival of large numbers of soldiers brought an increase in crime. There were reports of some of these crimes in the *Chelmsford Chronicle* in March 1802. Privates James Pincock and John Power of the 49th Regiment of Foot were jailed in Chelmsford for assaulting Hugh Pitts and stealing his silver watch and 2s on the road between Chelmsford and Broomfield. A few weeks later they were released after officers from their regiment spoke up for them praising their previous good character. It seems that the word of an officer went a long way at that time.

Once the Napoleonic Wars got underway again after the short spell of peace at the beginning of the nineteenth century, the army looked for somewhere to house its headquarters that was not too close to the coast. The government seemed to be taking invasion threats more seriously this time and built lines of defences. The Mildmay family, who owned a large house in Chelmsford, were not happy about the situation but also had the idea that the situation could be used to their advantage. By allowing the military to use Moulsham Hall they were released from the need to spend at least three months a year living at the hall, which had been a requirement until then. The agreement between the Mildmay family and the government only came after a series of letters between the two parties. The Mildmay family argued that they could not live in the house any longer due to robberies in the field next to the house, nine nights out of ten, the permanent barracks either side of the house and the threat of invasion.

Horse racing was popular in the area and continued until the 1930s. There was a rumour that after the war a member of the local Petre family obtained Marengo – Napoleon's famous white horse that he rode at Waterloo. If true, then it is possible that Marengo ran at Galleywood.

The Danbury camp had a long military history; the site had been an ancient hill fort that was again used by the military at a later date. The militia were also using the site as a camp well before the Napoleonic Wars as a Private Chorley Smith died there while stationed with the Royal Lancashire Volunteers in 1781.

Deaths among the soldiers were not just due to the war. A sergeant of the East Kent Militia was leading a working party from Danbury Camp in 1796. He had to use a wagon to return an injured man to the camp. Leaving his pregnant wife to return to the working party he overturned the wagon and suffered a fractured skull. He died a few days later and was buried in Danbury with full military honours.

The camp at Danbury was obviously well used, as an advertisement in the *Chelmsford Chronicle* in October 1801 called for a special meeting of the West Essex Volunteer Cavalry at the camp.

Another incident occurred at Danbury in 1803, which could have had widespread consequences. A messenger arrived to report that a fire had been seen near the coast that could have been an invasion-warning beacon. The troops at the camp were armed and there were plans to light the beacon, which would have started a line of warning fires being lit across the county. Before this happened however it was discovered that the fire near the coast was caused by someone burning weeds.

There were several attempts to increase militia numbers during the war. Often adverts were placed in newspapers for recruits. In July 1794, the Essex Militia wanted twenty men for the period of the war only. They advertised in the *Chelmsford Chronicle* for men less than thirty-five years of age, at least 5ft 5in tall (growing lads could be 5ft 4in). Applicants could apply at the Black Boy Inn, the White Hart at Moulsham or the Bull at Braintree. No one with more than one child in wedlock should apply. It also said that volunteers were likely to be drafted into the regular army.

The militia was run on a much stricter basis than the later Home Guard of the Second World War. There came to be a kind of draft for the militia and when the West Essex Militia, led by Colonel William Smyth, wanted men they stated that anyone not able to serve must pay 5s for a substitute. This was clearly unfair on the poorer men in society who did not have the money to buy themselves out of service, and some more liberal-minded ladies and gentlemen in London formed a society to raise money to pay for substitutes for industrious men with large families.

The Essex Light Dragoons wanted men willing to serve without going abroad. They offered six guineas for each recruit and high cavalry pay. Applications were to be made to Montague Burgoyne of Marks Hall, Harlow, or John Godsalve Crosse of Baddow near Chelmsford.

An extra incentive for recruits was a subscription from ladies and gentlemen to support the wives and children of any recruits who were injured in pursuing their duty. As another inducement to join the Light Dragoons, there was to be an ox roasted whole on Harlow Bush Common in May 1795. This was a token of approbation for the good behaviour of the regiment in their absence from Essex and a chance for their friends, and possible recruits, to see them. There was the added attraction of competitions with prizes. A silver laced hat to be run for by men, a fine shift to be run for by women and a medal for the parents who had brought up the most number of children with the least parochial assistance. Wagons to the ox roasting were run from Braintree, Chelmsford and Romford.

Enlisting in the militia seems to have been expected of most young men if they were not in the regular army. Once enrolled, however, getting out was not as easy. At the end of the eighteenth century, the *Chelmsford Chronicle* reported numerous cases of desertion, mostly with a reward offered. James Spurdon of Purleigh deserted from the West Essex Militia in 1794 and a reward of 20s was offered for his capture. The offer was repeated for a number of weeks along with a description of Spurdon.

As well as direct support for the war by serving in the militia, the population of Chelmsford, like other civilians throughout the country, had to pay for the conflict. A special rate was levied in 1795 to pay for the area's quota of men for the navy.

By 1813 the war in Europe looked as good as over and the threat of invasion was then non-existent. Many of the defences built in the area were pulled down and the new barracks were demolished in 1814. The relaxation turned out to be premature as Napoleon escaped from Elba the following year. The days of troops passing through the town returned as numerous regiments made their way through Chelmsford on their way to Harwich.

Other units, including artillery, passed through on their way to Tilbury, also disembarking to join Wellington. The victory at Waterloo brought a final end to the conflict and the rest of the defences were removed in 1815. The old barracks were not demolished until 1823 and left behind them a collection of huts populated by camp followers in what had become a very rough area.

Although the barracks were gone, troops still spent time in the town. The army became a means of control over the working class movements that petitioned for better conditions after the war. By 1829, as well as military there was also support from a force of 450 special constables, 100 of them mounted. There were many regular troops posted to Chelmsford after the French wars. In the 1860s there were also a number of permanent members of the West Essex Militia based in the Moulsham Barracks. The old jail was demolished in 1880 and the site was used as a parade ground.

COALHOUSE FORT

The building of the new Coalhouse Fort was begun in 1847, but Colonel Slade of the Royal Engineers thought that the building contractor had a troublesome character and the fort was not finished until 1855. Despite the long time it took to complete, the building did not last long and only six years later a new fort was built on the site.

The defences already at East Tilbury were well positioned but unable to be defended against modern weapons. The construction of three new forts on the Thames at that time suffered problems due to subsidence on the swampy ground. Two of the forts were in Kent and suffered more, which later led to larger guns intended for the Kent forts being sent to Coalhouse instead due to its firmer foundations. The fort's design went through several changes during its building. Gordon of Khartoum was involved towards the end of its construction.

Coalhouse Fort has a moat and ditch and there are several loopholes for small arms fire. Trees were planted round the building to help hide it from enemy view. One of the most striking features of the fort was its businesslike appearance. There are no elaborate gates such as the one at Tilbury Fort, just strong blocks of stone. By the end of the nineteenth century extra batteries had been added either side of the fort. One of these was just north of the church. All were armed with more modern guns which were able to fire armour-piercing shells to combat the development of armour-plated ships. By then, the fort had barracks for 200 men and a small hospital.

COLCHESTER

Colchester is one of the oldest, if not the oldest town in Britain, and has had a long and varied history – its military connections continuing up to the present day. It was fortified before the Romans arrived and was again walled after Boudicca and her tribe burnt it. Much of its early industry was based on cloth manufacture. This had mainly died out by the beginning of the nineteenth century when it reverted to being a market town. The cloth industry had been further damaged by many of the workers enlisting in the army, drawn by the large bounties on offer.

The Napoleonic Wars did in fact have an effect on most of the population. It led to the introduction of income tax. It also caused many families to lose their main breadwinner, as men went off to war and in many cases did not return. It was not only the army that was responsible for taking the men away. The Royal Navy was just as hungry for men to man their large ships. Press gangs operated in many towns taking unwilling hands off to sea. In 1795, the government also applied quotas of landsmen to be supplied to the Navy by towns or boroughs. These men were sought

Early military photographs were carefully posed, as in this example from the studio of Isaac Schofield in Mersea Road shows.

through advertisements in the local newspapers. Twenty guineas were offered to volunteers by Ongar and surrounding areas that needed to supply three men. The parish of All Saints also offered 20 guineas. Other areas of Colchester were having trouble finding their quota as they were offering £31 for volunteers to go to sea, and the advertisement was running for some time in the *Chelmsford Chronicle* despite the large amount on offer.

Although the building of barracks may have cut the number of soldiers billeted in inns, it did not stop the troops from being customers. Two new inns were opened close to the gates just after the barracks themselves were completed. Most inns at the time were owned by breweries and other organisations, and owner-occupiers were rare. The Evening Gun in Colchester was let for £60 a year in 1799, but had an annual turnover of more than £5,000.

One early effect of a garrison in the town was to spread panic through the area after rumours of an invasion were started by a sergeant at Colchester. Sergeant Thomas Bell of the North York Militia added a paragraph to a written order by a Major Bolling that told a soldier to bring in men from harvest work in the locality. Bell wrote that the French would be dining at Ipswich by the following Sunday.

It was reported that the ensuing panic caused by this rumour could have been fatal to some. The death penalty was called for, or at least severe corporal punishment for Bell. The word of commanding officers seem to have had a great influence however as when Bell's Commanding Officer spoke up for him describing his previous good character he was let off. Bell claimed that the statement had been a joke. He was sent to St Osyth on a Sunday to apologise to the local population as they left the church.

The arrival of a permanent garrison in the town also led to a celebrity visitor and an event that was at the forefront of medical treatment at that time. Dr Edward Jenner was invited to Colchester by the Commander in Chief, the Duke of York, in 1800. Jenner had a few years previously discovered that milkmaids who caught cowpox from their herds never caught smallpox. Smallpox was a big killer at the time and there had been previous outbreaks in Colchester. Jenner had carried out an experiment and infected his gardener's eight-year-old son with cowpox. He then exposed him to smallpox. The boy did not develop the disease, which seemed to prove Jenner's theory. At the Duke of York's invitation, Dr Jenner inoculated the entire 85th regiment with cowpox.

The arrival of large numbers of soldiers had an immediate effect on the prosperity of the area as the production of food to supply the barracks encouraged growth in the local market gardening industry. This did much to stimulate an economy, which was based on very little industry. It was not just local food growers – who found helpers in harvest time among idle soldiers – who profited from the army's arrival. Provision merchants, shopkeepers and brewers all did well, not only because of the army's arrival but also through the increase in the town's population.

By the time the barracks were built the prestige of farmers had risen in society. Many of the farms that went up for sale locally were bought by men from London, and it was not just high profits from producing food for the troops that tempted them. When farms were advertised, selling points could be that they were situated in sporting areas or were well stocked with game. Farmhouses were often described as suitable for genteel families. What London buyers were seeking was Essex estates, and improved transport links to London made this more tempting.

The new gentlemen farmers and those who made money from industry were by then accepted into Essex society. They also mixed with officers from the new barracks who came from the same social class.

As well as the barracks in the town there was also a camp during the summer months at nearby Lexden. This was mainly used by the militia, although in August 1795 the third Regiment of Light Dragoons, commanded by a Colonel Blake, were stationed there. The area contained the Lexden Tumulus, which was thought to contain the grave of the last Trinovantian king of the area, Addedomaras.

Propaganda may have been a more common weapon in later wars but an article in the *Chelmsford Chronicle* as early as 1796 entitled 'Common sense to common man' was an obvious attempt to raise morale and to warn against French tricks. It stated that the French, unable to win the war by arms, were trying to win by arts. The article warned that as invasion threats had been in vain they were sending spies and agents to England to work on the minds of the population.

Not everything about the army's arrival improved the town, there were also disadvantages, but these were more to do with the threat of invasion than with the barracks. The threat seemed especially strong in 1803 when hostilities resumed after a spell of peace. The Butter Market was walled in to make a guardhouse. Many local residents left the area and moved away from what had by then become a front-line town.

Between 1792 and 1815 there were over 150 barracks built in the country. The majority of these were in the Midlands and the north. Some believe that this was because these areas were where the population was the unhappiest and most likely to suffer unrest. The presence of a large group of soldiers was a deterrent to any groups hoping to start any trouble.

Essex was not free of public disturbance problems. Enclosures of land were one action that had brought hardship to the local poor and there were numerous protests over this and other problems during and after the Napoleonic Wars. These were mainly held by working men who had no jobs. There were however protests by the more wealthy members of society, and at the end of the eighteenth century there was strong resistance in Colchester to enclosures on Mile End Heath.

These demonstrations often resulted in the military themselves being used to quell public disturbances. In 1816, machine breakers were at large in Halstead. Unemployed farm workers broke machines, which they blamed for their unemployment. When the ringleaders were arrested their supporters took over the town. When the local yeomanry arrived they were driven off by a mob throwing stones. After that dragoons were called out from Colchester and put an end to the riot.

The horror displayed by the upper classes at the crimes committed by the working classes was obvious from newspaper reports. Incidents of arson were described as 'Disgraceful even to the state of barbarism.' One report went on to claim that highwaymen's and even traitors' actions could be understood, but not those of protesters. The writer argued that all classes had suffered during the recent difficulties, not just the poor.

There had, in fact, been a change in the economic position of the poor in Essex during the early nineteenth century. As the previously poorer northern and midland areas became involved in the industrial revolution, wages began to rise, while areas with less industry and a mainly rural economy such as Essex had increasing levels of poor relief. Of course, as the arrival of the army had increased prosperity during the war, it also dealt the local economy a savage blow once the war ended and the troops left. Along with the rest of the nation, Colchester had quite a rough time.

The increased prosperity of the town during the war led to improvements that had not been possible before, such as the building of the Theatre Royal in 1812. No doubt the new building was as popular with the officers from the barracks as it was with the local dignitaries. Fashionable life in the town was no doubt enriched by the presence of officers in their colourful uniforms. Many of the officers from the barracks enjoyed the popular Victorian pastime of amateur dramatics and appeared in shows at the theatre. They also started the military tradition of raising money for local charities. In April 1856, officers of the Essex Rifles Militia Company staged a benefit night at the theatre in aid of the local hospital. In 1856, several officers from the Guards took parts in 'A Sheep in Wolf's Clothing' at the theatre in aid of the County Asylum at Brentwood. Despite its popularity with the troops, the theatre was not looked upon as respectable by many local residents. There was a plan to turn the building into a soldiers' home but this never happened. A soldiers' home did however open in the town in 1873: it was started by a Miss Daniels of the Soldiers' Mission at Aldershot.

Although Colchester did not suffer from the same health problems as those barracks built in the Essex marshes, the arrival of the army did bring its own health issues.

In October 1863, a hurricane caused severe damage to the new cavalry barracks while they were still being built. The army later bought Middlemarch Farm to replace Wivenhoe Park, which had been used for manoeuvres. Rifle ranges were also added to the site. By 1862 there were several camp schools for the children of the soldiers.

Although not directly involved in the American Civil War, many officers from the Colchester Barracks went to America to act as observers. There were also numerous volunteers from Britain, including Essex, who went and fought in the war, on both sides.

HARWICH

The road from Harwich carried one of the counties first stagecoach services from the early eighteenth century. There were two coaches a week, which took a day and a half to reach Harwich from London. By the time of the Napoleonic Wars the journey time had been cut to ten hours.

Not all passengers arriving from the continent wanted to use public transport. There were attempts to attract the custom of wealthier travellers by some inhabitants of the town. For example, £200 was spent making the Three Cups Inn more 'genteel'. It was also possible to hire private coaches at the inn to travel to London. No doubt a fashionable inn also did good trade with officers from the barracks a few years later.

The East Essex were at Harwich in 1782. The Hertford Militia had been camped there in 1796 and there is no doubt that the Harwich military camp was as big as the other summer military camps in Essex.

In 1797, Brigadier General Sir John Moore, the hero of Corunna, was on a tour of inspection of Essex. He thought that the county was the most likely place for an invasion attempt, especially the Clacton area. He was in Harwich in October and also visited Landguard Fort. He then went on to Clacton and, after inspecting the area, decided that the eight miles between Walton Gap and Clacton Wick were the most likely spot for an enemy landing.

A Military Memoir for the defence of the Eastern District was written in 1798 and also pointed out this area as the most vulnerable spot. The view was that the counties directly north of Essex were unsuitable for invasion as was the area between Harwich cliffs and the Naze. The report also stated that as the principal fleet in the area lay off Yarmouth that a squadron of ships should be left at Hollesley Bay in Suffolk, which could then reach the danger area quickly if needed.

There was a suggestion that a ship and four gunboats should be moored in Harwich harbour which could also support the Clacton area. The report pointed out that the entrance to Harwich port for ships was too close to the Suffolk bank for defences on the Essex side of the river to have any effect on them. Land-based defences should therefore be left to Landguard Fort.

In 1799, ships carrying wounded from the war in Europe landed at Harwich. Hospitals for them had been set up at Mill House, the Three Cups Inn and the White Hart.

In other towns near the coast emergency plans were made on what to do in the event of an invasion. Harwich was no different. One ingenious plan was that the Low Lighthouse would be demolished and a false portable one erected in a different place, thus causing enemy ships to run aground. There were also plans to destroy other lighthouses and to cut adrift marker buoys to further confuse an invasion force.

Another report on Essex defences was written in 1805, which was not as confident about Landguard Fort being a sufficient defence for the harbour. As Harwich was the most important harbour in Essex it was seen as vital that it did not fall into enemy hands. The report suggested that there should be three new batteries: at Shotley Point, Walton Ferry and a heavy sea battery under the lighthouse.

Harwich had often been used as the port for wounded soldiers returning from the war in Europe. One of these incidents was the famous repatriation into the town of many of the men from the ill-fated Walcheren expedition. Forty thousand men had been sent to the island in 1810 to attack Antwerp, including many from nearby Weeley Barracks. Over 7,000 of them died of fever and the expedition was abandoned. Many of the men died after returning to England via Harwich and some are buried in All Saints churchyard.

A tablet inside the church is dedicated to the memory of Lieutenant Colonel Graham Donaldson, who was one of those who died after returning home, and was placed there by officers of the 1st Foot Guards. The west window of the church was donated by Kaiser Wilhelm II in 1900, in memory of the German soldiers who took part in the Walcheren expedition alongside the British. There is also a gate to the church donated by Queen Victoria commemorating the same event.

There was a large garrison at Harwich throughout the Napoleonic Wars, acting as both a barrier against any invasion and to guard the shipyards. A number of large warships with up to seventy-four guns were built in the local dockyards.

After the war, the size of the barracks were scaled down and most were demolished a few years afterwards. A garrison, however, remained in Harwich, for in 1826 a Mr Clark delivered two tons of straw to Harwich Barracks.

Although the arrival of troops in many Essex towns led to an increase in prosperity, this does not seem to have been the case in Harwich. Although a few may have profited from the barracks and its occupants, Harwich remained quite a poor area. Its main income seemed to derive from the Post Office packets, which sailed to Northern Europe with letters and passengers. This declined with the invention of steamships. Fishing was also a thriving industry in the eighteenth century, but the number of fishing boats declined from around eighty to nearer ten by the early nineteenth century.

During the war there had been calls by the local population to improve street lighting and provide proper paving. There was not even a decent supply of water in the town and many still relied on collecting rainwater for their use.

The fiftieth anniversary of George III's reign was celebrated during the conflict. A meal was provided by the corporation for the poor. The number of needy had multiplied sharply during the war years as food prices had risen.

Despite the problems and the poverty, the end of the war and Napoleon's detention in Elba was celebrated. A meal was again supplied on the green for over 700 poor people; this was followed by games and fireworks, and the burning of an effigy of Napoleon. The corporation were not as generous after the final battle of the war. They gave only £10 for the relief of widows and orphans of those killed at Waterloo.

When one considers that the population of Harwich was not very large, less than 3,000 at the beginning of the nineteenth century, then 700 poor people was a large percentage of the overall population. The cost of poor relief in the fifty years leading up to the war had spiralled in both Harwich and Dovercourt. The effects on public order in response to the condition of the poor were a serious worry.

The Harwich Volunteers had made plans to deal with any public disorder during the war. The presence of the military in many towns was not only a means of defending the country from foreign enemies, but also dealt with the rise in public disquiet after the war.

There were widespread events of machine breaking and demonstrations in the county after the war. In one event, over 200 labourers paraded through Ramsey when a fire broke out. Arson was a favourite tactic of demonstrators. The military from Harwich were called out to deal with the demonstration, and arrived with the mayor and wealthy men from the town. These revolts were largely seen as demonstrations by the poor against the rich.

One of the largest industries in the area was the production of cement. The Board of Ordnance actually owned a cement mill in the town from 1818. For most of its life it was let out at £500 per year. The board also gave permission to a Mr Allder to dig stone from the cliffs of Beacon Hill at a price of £300 per year. Digging around the site of Beacon Hill must have had some effect on the defences built on the summit. A similar request to dig stone from the site in the sixteenth century had been refused for exactly that reason.

When there was another revolution in France in 1848, many believed that the Chartist movements could lead to similar events occurring in England. This led to many meetings of protest groups being cancelled by the authorities as illegal.

A fresh invasion scare began after the latest French problems and this led to the re-arming of the Martello towers in the area with larger guns.

By 1848 the redoubt had a garrison of eighty men. There was also a Royal Ordnance Depot near the High Lighthouse. This was used to store ammunition and guns for the batteries in Harwich and the Martello towers in the area, as by then Weeley Barracks, the former home of the Martello garrisons, was gone.

Beacon Hill Battery was built on a site that had been used as a defensive position in the past. One of Henry VIII's blockhouses was built there in the 1540s. There were further fortifications added at the time of the Spanish Armada. The site was also used in the Napoleonic Wars.

In 1863 a Conservancy Board was set up to take control of Harwich Harbour. This took control away from the Admiralty and the local Corporations although they each had a member on the Board. This was due to the fear that Landguard Point was extending into the mouth of the estuary due to a build up of shingle, and could make entrance into Harwich difficult. It was felt that the control of such a board would make the work of dealing with this problem simpler

MALDON

At the beginning of the eighteenth century Maldon was still in the main a market town, but also had up to a hundred ships a year calling at its port. The majority of these took farm produce to London but some also brought coal from the North of England. There were also a number of small boats bringing chalk into the port, which was used to improve the soil on farms. These boats would then return with loads of grain.

By the beginning of the nineteenth century there were over 500 ships a year arriving at the port and it had become the town's main source of income. Because of this most locals were against the idea of improving river links to Chelmsford, as this would mean a loss of trade for the port. When a canal was finally built to link the River Chelmer with the Blackwater, it bypassed Maldon and went to Heybridge. This led to a decline in business at Maldon's port and a return to its main business as a market town.

In keeping with its military past there were also barracks at Maldon. They were built at the end of the eighteenth century and lasted until after Napoleon's defeat. There had been a lot of rebuilding taking place in the town towards the end of the eighteenth century. Many large houses had been built with profits from its port. It gave the town a more modern look by the time the Essex Militia Cavalry (whose barracks were built in London Road) were stationed there between 1800 and 1833. Many of the new houses of the period were built by officers from the barracks who preferred to live in the luxury they were accustomed to rather than basic conditions in barracks. Two other buildings thought to have been used as barracks were built among some ancient fortified earthworks which were part of Eadwards Burh, built during his war against the Vikings. The earthworks may also have been used as a defence for the new camp. The barracks were in the parish of All Saints.

The location of the barracks at Maldon was no doubt partly due to the danger of invaders using the rivers close by. The view was that the Colne was probably too difficult to navigate for an invading force. The Crouch could be navigated by soundings only and the Blackwater was only known well enough to be navigated by local fishermen.

The poor levels of health that were present in the coastal areas of Essex were also rife in Maldon. The illness that struck the area in 1806 was however more serious than the fevers that struck at Weeley a few years later. At least six people died of smallpox in the town in that year.

The 3rd Battalion First Regiment of Foot, Royal Scots, spent some time at Maldon. In 1809 some of the battalion's sick and wounded came home from Spain after fighting against Napoleon. The sick and wounded sailed back on HMS *Radcliffe*. They spent time at Chelmsford before returning to Spain. The next year the injured were sent back again but this time were stationed at Maldon.

As with other barracks, there was obviously some attraction between the young men of the forces and the young ladies of the town. In 1809 a marriage took place between Mary Payne, daughter of John, a merchant of Maldon, and Captain Miller Clifford of the 28th Regiment of Foot, who were by then stationed at Colchester.

Although there was no problem with officers marrying, it was frowned upon within the ranks. Only six men per company were allowed to marry and bring their wives into barracks. This often led to men marrying without leave, whose new wives were not permitted to live with them in camp. This led to many tearful partings at the dockside when regiments were posted overseas, with wives not being allowed to travel with their husbands.

Although business in the port may have declined by the time the barracks were built, the previous century had been a time of expansion for the town. It was a popular place to visit for Londoners. Race meetings at Potman Marsh were well attended, and balls were held every evening after the racing. Maldon was one of the few Essex towns to have a bookshop in the mid-eighteenth century and there was also a book and print sale at the King's Head Inn towards the end of the century.

There were nineteen inns in Maldon by 1741. A few years later, travelling theatre companies began to visit the town and perform plays. The King's Head was a popular inn with farmers who were improving their social status at the time. The inn was also used by Whigs in 1810 to celebrate Charles Fox's birthday. Fox had been one of the leading English politicians in favour of the French Revolution. Support for him dwindled as the war progressed. Another popular inn was the Blue Boar, used for municipal meetings and as a headquarters of the volunteer cavalry during the war.

As well as the better-off residents there were also a large number of artisans living in the town. In 1784, over half of the men of Maldon fit to serve in the militia were from this class. Maldon must have been quite a civilised town for the officers of the troops who were stationed there during the lifetime of the barracks.

In many other Essex towns with military barracks, the soldiers were used as a means of public control. This was especially true after the war when the Chartist movement became strong in the area. The inhabitants of Maldon were however more enlightened in their thinking. The local corporation tried means other than force to control the poor. Many rich women in the area began a subscription to provide the poor with necessities during the most troubled times. They hoped that this would make the needy think twice before joining reform movements because of the gratitude they felt towards their better-off neighbours.

Another scheme tried in the area was enrolling the poor into Provident Societies, where even a few pence invested gave them a stake in something. The Mayor of Maldon did not think twice about using this as another means of keeping the local poor out of Chartist groups. He told them that involvement in such groups could put their investment in danger.

An auction of the land on which the barracks was based was held in 1816. The auction also comprised of the furniture, utensils and fixtures of the barracks. This included sixty cauldrons of coal, and building materials. The land itself consisted of 6¾ acres and was noted to have four wells, which, due to shortages of fresh water in the area where many still relied on rainwater for their supplies of drinking water, greatly enhanced the property. There was also one building left on the site. It was built of timber and had been the officers' accommodation and mess. It was described as suitable as the home of a gentleman.

Although there were barracks being sold off at the time, there were still many in existence. In the same edition of the *Star* newspaper that advertised the sale of Maldon Barracks there was an advertisement placed by the Commissary in Chief at St Georges Street, London. It asked for tenders to be sent, in sealed envelopes, to supply beef and mutton to land forces in cantonments, quarters and barracks. One of the county's listed as including these sites was Essex.

The closure of the barracks did not signal the end of the town's involvement with the military – a company of Essex Regiment Volunteers with their own band was based in the town from 1876.

PURFLEET

The small village of Purfleet was once a popular place with the affluent from London until the nineteenth century. They would often travel down by boat for a pleasant evening visit by the river. The Purfleet Hotel later became the Royal Hotel and was a popular retreat for these visitors. It is likely that Bram Stoker may have been one of these visitors before giving his famous vampire, Count Dracula, a home in the town.

Purfleet's most important connection with the military originated in the form of a gunpowder magazine. The magazine was built alongside the Royal Hotel on the banks of the Thames. It was not the only magazine to be built along the banks of the river or in Essex. The first in the county was built in the mid-sixteenth century in Waltham Abbey. The River Lea was used to transport barges full of gunpowder down to the Thames and later these came to Woolwich and Purfleet.

The government magazine at Woolwich was built in 1694. It would take deliveries from other mills and store, test and distribute the powder. The danger of having such a potentially explosive building in the area led to the local population petitioning for its removal, especially after an explosion actually occurred.

There was another magazine built at Creekmouth in Barking in 1719 when the local magistrates gave permission for the building of a magazine on the site. It was probably at that time the only building in the area which was some distance from the town itself. The magazine was only owned by the government for about fifty years. Once Purfleet magazine was complete the Barking site was sold to a private buyer, and changed hands on numerous occasions during its lifetime. It was still, however, under military guard while privately owned.

The Barking magazine was big enough to store over 100 tons of gunpowder, which was not a problem while it stood alone by the bank of the Thames and Barking Creek. It was a different matter, however, once other factories and houses were built in the vicinity.

Purfleet was an ideal position as a replacement for Woolwich. It was close to the Thames so convenient for transport and sparsely populated so would not put a large civilian population at risk. Planning began in 1760, and once complete took over the duties that had been carried out at Woolwich: testing and storing powder before shipping it to both army and navy. The government finally acquired Waltham Abbey gunpowder factory from the owner, John Walton, in 1787.

The building of Purfleet magazine caused immediate problems for some local residents. The Sheriff of Essex was ordered to attend with a jury at the Angel Inn, Ilford, at the end of 1760 to deal with the purchase of the land needed for the magazine. There were several houses standing on the main street through Purfleet that had to be purchased and demolished. There were also houses backing onto Back Lane. As well as these houses, the government also purchased the stables belonging to the Crown Inn, a nearby bricklayer's yard and a mill. They also bought several fields surrounding the buildings, including Old Cliff Field, also known by the more colourful name of Dead Man's Hole. The total cost of demolishing the old magazine at Woolwich, buying land at Purfleet and building the new magazine, a guardhouse and barracks was £15,000.

An Act of Parliament in 1772 made it unlawful to manufacture gunpowder without a licence. The act also ruled that magazines or gunpowder factories on the Thames had to be below Blackwall.

Worries over the safety of the magazine led to a famous visitor to Purfleet in August 1772. A committee of the Royal Society was directed by the government to examine how the magazine could be protected from lightning. One of the committee had already visited the site at the request of the Board of Ordnance; Benjamin Franklin was a member of the society and he happened to be in England at the time. He suggested that pointed lightning rods, which had been in use in America for twenty years, be fixed to the buildings.

Another member of the committee, Mr Wilson, an artist, argued with Franklin. He believed that rods should be blunt as pointed ones attract lightning. In Franklin's view this was the objective of a rod. When lightening did strike the magazine in 1777, there was some damage to the building. It seemed that the conductor had not attracted the lightning, as Franklin believed it would. This restarted the debate about what type of conductors should be used. It would seem that many of Wilson's supporters were more influenced by politics than science. Franklin had, after all, had a hand in the American Revolution.

The officer's house at Purfleet, 1875. The man in civilian clothes is Captain Robson of the Royal Artillery. The woman in the house is Mrs Robson. The man in uniform is H. Barron from the Royal Artillery.

In 1794 William Kitchenham deserted from Purfleet. He was a member of the East Kent Militia posted at the magazine as a guard. A reward of one guinea above the normal 20*s* was offered for his capture. In the same year William James, the storekeeper at Purfleet, died.

Although there had been no accidents on the site of the magazine, there were some close by. In 1796, a nearby public house owned by Mr Whitbread was burned to the ground. The building was only 300yds from the magazine.

A further stretch of land was obtained in 1809 to allow the road to be widened. However, instead of buying this land, it was exchanged for other land with Samuel Whitbread, a local landowner.

There were five magazine buildings about 50yds from the bank of the river at Purfleet. Each building held over 10,000 barrels of powder. They were built to withstand explosions and the men working in them were supplied with special equipment and uniforms. The area of about 25 acres had a protective wall around it. There was also a large house built on the hill above the magazine for the storekeeper.

It was not only local regiments that were based at Purfleet: this is a carefully posed photograph of the 2nd Battalion the Buffs, Royal East Kent Regiment, in 1885.

In 1839 another accident close to Purfleet put the magazine at risk. A collier brig, the *Swallow*, caught fire at Gallions Reach. It happened while the crew were asleep and although they escaped the ship went aground on the Essex bank of the river, fortunately not close enough to the magazine to cause a problem, but the coal in the hold caught fire and burnt strongly for hours after the ship was destroyed.

The rifle ranges at Purfleet were also well used. In 1866, the 1st Middlesex Artillery held their annual carbine prize meeting at Purfleet. There were prizes ranging between £3 and £10. First prize was won by a Corporal Meens. There were also consolation prizes for women.

Fear of accidents at gunpowder sites led to an article in the *Penny Illustrated* newspaper in January 1868. It gave a detailed account of how the magazine was run to allay public worries. Some details would, however, have defeated this object. The article stated that the amount of powder stored was enormous and that an accident could lay half of Kent, Middlesex and Surrey in ruins. The failure to mention what would happen to Essex points to a thought too horrific to contemplate.

A similar article had been published in the *Engineer* four years earlier. It stated that if Purfleet blew up it would take the roofs off houses as far away as Gravesend and Woolwich, which was where the original magazine had been. It would also have broken the windows of most houses in London. The article did however point out that no accidents from the building of the magazine had occurred to date. It also stated that when first built, it was in a remote area. By 1868 however there was a village close by and many fine villas.

The objective of the magazine was that every atom of gunpowder made at Waltham Abbey, Dartford, Faversham or Hounslow was either approved and put in store at Purfleet or refused and sent back. The site was therefore open every day, receiving or sending out powder. During the Crimean War the magazine worked all day and all night, not that it made much difference to the gloom inside the windowless buildings.

The magazine had a garrison of two officers and eighty men, as well as several coopers, clerks and storekeepers. There was also a tailor who made flannel dresses worn by all staff and a shoemaker who made soft leather shoes. The chief of the establishment was a Mr Cleave who showed any visitors to the magazine around himself. All of the workers lived on the site along with their wives and children.

Apart from the five magazines there was also an examining room in which powder was tested for dust and dirt. The powder was then tested in a mortar. The quality was defined by how far the solid shot from the weapon was thrown.

Not all the workers at the magazine were members of the armed forces. One of the civilian employees at the site became a celebrity at the end of the eighteenth century. Jack Watts had been a soldier and was a witness to an incident where a soldier was sentenced to 800 lashes and died under the punishment. The man who ordered the flogging was Governor Wall, while in command of an island off the coast of Africa. It was to be twenty years after the incident before Wall returned to England and finally stood trial. Watts was a witness and after being found guilty Wall was hung at Tyburn. In a strange twist to the story, Jack Watts later hanged himself in a wood close to the magazine. It later became known locally as Jack Watt's wood.

By the late nineteenth century security was being tightened. Between 1870 and 1873 new concrete huts were added for extra troops. The garrison then had up to eighty artillerymen stationed there. Extra troops arrived in 1878 when there were rumours of a suspected attack on the site by Fenians. As well as extra troops, police were also involved and all civilian staff were enlisted to help guard the magazines.

The site did not escape from both natural and man-made disasters despite increased security. In 1874, a barge carrying ammunition, oil and powder caught fire on the River Thames. The crew managed to get the barge across the river to the Kent bank, but with burning oil floating across the water there were a few worrying hours for the workers at the magazine. At around the same time there was an incident at the military infant school on the site. A 5-year-old girl was murdered and the teacher at the barracks, Richard Coutis, who was a member of the artillery, was found guilty of the crime. He was later hanged.

In 1895 a severe spell of cold weather caused the River Thames to freeze over. This meant that all powder had to be brought in and sent out by wagon. This included the powder from several barges frozen in the River Lea on their way to Purfleet from Waltham Abbey.

Conditions for the soldiers at the site must have improved at the camp when a new canteen was built in 1873. For the first few years, tenants who were all ex-army men, ran it. It was then taken over by the Middlesex Regiment who ran it until the man they put in charge was involved in some financial irregularities. He committed suicide by drowning himself near the Royal Hotel. The canteen then went back to the tenant system until the First World War.

Following the tradition of keeping dangerous explosive production out of the way on the bank of the Thames, an explosives factory was built further along the river on the marshes stretching from Stanford-le-Hope to Holehaven Creek in 1895. It was built by Kynoch & Co. and employed over 600 workers making explosives for the South African War. It had its own school and shop and became known as Kynochtown. It continued production throughout the First World War and finally closed in 1919, before becoming an oil refinery.

SHOEBURYNESS

For most of its history, Shoebury was a quiet and remote village, which made it the ideal site for the army and suited their purposes – firing live shells was not the thing to do in a highly populated area. Although its remote position was an advantage, there were drawbacks.

The Essex marshes were not the healthiest of places for habitation, especially for women who suffered badly from the malaria that was still rife along the Thames coast. It was one of the last places in Britain where malaria-carrying mosquitoes survived. Daniel Defoe, writing in 1724, had noticed that the fever was more lethal to women. He said that it was not unusual for a man living in the marshes to have up to fifteen wives during his lifetime. Another reason for this high mortality rate in women may have been that many of the women came from healthier areas and were not as immune to the disease as those who had lived there all their lives.

Above: The swampy ground at Shoeburyness made it the ideal place to practice bridge building, as this pontoon bridge shows.

Right: A different type of bridge, a Double Truss.

The name Shoeburyness is actually an administrative area consisting of North and South Shoebury and was a result of the Post Office calling the army camp by the name Shoeburyness. This was not something that some locals were happy about.

The population had not grown much in the hundred years before the artillery arrived. North Shoebury had a population of 115 families in 1763, which had only grown to 202 families by the beginning of the nineteenth century. South Shoebury was even smaller with sixty-nine families in 1763, reaching 101 families by the end of the century.

Left: Some of the guns at Shoeburyness were very large and needed elaborate feats of engineering to move them, as this large assembly shows.

Below: The weight of the gun held by the pulley system must have been immense. The close proximity of the men shows that they must have had confidence in their ability.

The 22-ton gun made by Horsfalls of Liverpool and sent to Shoeburyness for testing.

There were several strange types of weapons tested during the nineteenth century as inventors came up with new ideas to cause havoc among the enemy. One of the largest cast-iron guns made at that time spent eleven years at the site until it was moved to Tilbury Fort in 1862. It weighed 22 tons.

The real advance in the importance of the Shoebury site was the development of armoured ships. To combat these modern marvels it was necessary to find workable amour-piercing shells. As the move to develop this ammunition became more pronounced, guns began to become more complicated. This led to an expansion in the size of the site from 50 to 200 acres. When the armoured ship *La Gloire* was launched by the French in 1860, Palmerston set up a Royal Commission which recommended nineteen new forts and fifty-seven new batteries around the coast. That was despite the French being our allies in the Crimea.

The development of armour-piercing shells was reported in the *Illustrated London News* on Boxing Day 1863. The report was illustrated with a picture of Sir William Armstrong's 200lb rifled gun, and went into detail about how the gun was made and the three types of shells it could fire: solid, hollow with a charge of gunpowder or a segment shell for use against troops, filled with small pieces of iron. The newspaper also had a picture of a floating target with 4½in of iron plate fixed on 18ins of teak backed with another ¾in of iron. A shell from the gun pierced the target at 1,020yds. The fact that the pictures were on the front page of the newspaper showed the wide level of interest in such experiment at Shoeburyness. It also showed how the preoccupation with secrecy over military matters was a long way off in the future.

New buildings were added when the camp expanded, including a church in 1866 and bungalows for married men. Any expansion of the artillery site was opposed by local fishermen. Not only were the areas taken over no longer available to locals but they also argued that there were no longer any winkles, cockles or mussels on the foreshore. The view in the community was that marine life had been scared off by the explosions of shells.

Until this time married quarters were very rare. The few men allowed to marry had to live with their wives in the barracks with the other men. The corner system, as it was known, had been criticised as indecent and by this period it was also realised that not allowing men to marry encouraged them to visit prostitutes. This led to more cases of sexually transmitted diseases.

During experiments with ironclad targets, this one was called the La Gloire Target after the French ironclad of the time. It was easily pierced by Sir William Armstrong's large shunt guns.

There seems to have been a very relaxed attitude towards the artillery experiments at Shoeburyness.

In 1891, a circular was sent out by the Archbishop of Canterbury concerning the pitiable condition of deserted wives who had married soldiers without leave (marrying without the commanding officer's permission). The archbishop advised clergy in garrison towns to dissuade both soldiers and women from marrying without leave. He also had the idea of using military chapels for weddings so officers could keep a check on just who was getting married.

The rules on marriage were very unfair. All warrant officers could marry, as could all non-commissioned officers above the rank of sergeant. Half of all sergeants could marry but only one in every twenty-five from other ranks. The archbishop also pointed out that it was possible to deduct three pence a day from the wages of soldiers who married without leave, to support their wives. Commanding officers were instructed by the Queen's Regulations to sedulously discourage the improvident marriage of soldiers and to explain to the men the inevitable trouble and distress that must ultimately arise.

The arrival of married quarters led to a distinction between the wives of different ranks: there were officers and their ladies, non-commissioned officers and their wives and privates and their women. Apart from the ladies, other women in barracks were expected to work and did the regiment's washing and sewing. The wives of non-commissioned officers did the officers' washing.

A report on the barracks described the buildings and the conditions the men had to live under. The barracks were of two floors with four rooms on each level holding twelve men. This seemed to be the most common pattern for barrack buildings at the time. The rooms were described as well ventilated but also warm. The camp was able to accommodate over 700 men but rarely had more than 500. Of these, around 200 were permanent gunnery school staff, the rest were made up of various regiments that came and went.

It was noted that there were washing facilities but that the men often bathed in the sea in summer. In winter things must have been a bit more difficult. Four hours of drill took place per day in winter and five hours in the summer. As well as a library, there was also a bowling alley and regular lectures and concerts. Although, like much of the Essex coastline, Shoebury had been quite unhealthy due to the swamps, by the time of the report much of the land had been drained, creating a much healthier atmosphere for the troops.

An orchestra was formed at the camp in the mid-nineteenth century that lasted until the First World War. The orchestra put on concerts for the garrison and for locals in a large tent at the base and in Southend Public Hall. There was also a drama group which performed plays. These were at first put on in the drill hall and an entrance fee was charged to pay for heaters. In 1884, a large portable building was erected just outside the camp, which was used as a concert hall and theatre.

There were good sports facilities at the camp and several sports teams played against local civilian sides. The base football team played against Thames Ironworks, who were the predecessors of the football club West Ham United. The Ironworks also had a hand in building the kind of armoured ships that the experiments at Shoebury were aimed at destroying.

In 1873, a military tramway was built on the site to link three piers and to transport stores brought in by river. Although this was in fact a railway, it was called a tramway because of confusing legislation at the time. The line was extended to the New Ranges in 1890. It was again extended to Havengore Point in 1890.

A public right of way through the site was closed in the nineteenth century, as it was getting too dangerous for members of the public, who could wander in at will to watch the experiments. Often tips were offered to the soldiers to explain what the experiments were for. Boats would also land on the beach full of day-trippers, who would then want to watch experiments or would stop them altogether because their boats were in the way.

The presence of soldiers was never popular with civilians. The growing popularity of Southend as a place to visit was causing problems due to immorality. In some cases it was believed that it was soldiers from the barracks who were mainly responsible, not the visitors.

SOUTHEND

Leigh-on-Sea was at one time a well-known naval refitting base used by Admiral Blake in the seventeenth century. The area was also known for shipbuilding. The *Port Mahoud*, a man of war lost off Shoeburyness in 1716, was built there (hopefully not on its maiden voyage which would not have taken it very far).

The end of the eighteenth century was a period of expansion in the town when the well-off began to visit the new seaside resort of Southend. Of course, one disadvantage of this was the fact that England was again at war with France at that time, and it was hardly a tempting proposition to visit the seaside when a French invasion force could arrive at any moment.

Another event that must have deterred visitors was when ringleaders from the Nore Mutiny used the Ship Hotel as one of their headquarters in May and June 1797. Although there was no trouble involving the mutineers, their presence and the fact that the government were massing troops along the Thames in case of conflict with them did deter visitors to the town.

As well as royal visitors, Southend also received some well-known names. One in particular was the mistress of England's most famous sailor, Lady Hamilton, whose

Landings by volunteer forces were often carried out in coastal areas during training. This one at Southend in June 1863 shows an invading force landing in boats being opposed by infantry and artillery on land.

visits to the town often lasted around a month between 1803 and 1805. On one occasion she gave a ball in honour of Nelson and the guests included the local naval officers. There were even rumours that Nelson himself visited the town but there is no clear evidence of this.

Southend, along with other seaside towns, was used as a practice landing site for the armed forces. On Whit Monday 1863, a large seaborne attack was launched by militia units. Large numbers of troops were landed by boat onto the beaches where they attacked a large defending force consisting of artillery and infantry.

ST VINCENT

This tiny hamlet in the village of South Weald has a name that connects it to a sea battle which took place on the other side of the world. The name originates from a man named John Jervis, who came to live at a large house in the area called Rocketts at around the turn of the nineteenth century. At this time Jervis was better known as the Lord St Vincent due to his part in a naval battle that took place on 14 February 1797. A naval squadron under the command of Admiral Sir John Jervis, as he was then known, came across a Spanish Fleet; newly allied to the French the Spanish were about to attack Barbados and St Vincent. The Spanish fleet was defeated and Jervis became an Earl.

After his retirement from naval life, Jervis came to Essex but it was a far from retirement into obscurity. Social life at Rocketts must have been a revelation to the local population, with visitors from the royal family including George IV and William IV. Perhaps an even more famous visitor was Lord St Vincent's great friend, Lord Nelson.

It seems that Lord St Vincent was known for being outspoken and was not too timid to criticise Nelson's relationship with Lady Hamilton. His quick temper led to a dispute with the local vicar, which ended with the lord swearing never to enter the local church again. This promise was kept even after his death, for he was buried in Staffordshire, his birthplace, in 1823.

TILBURY FORT

There was obviously no love lost between the men of the two counties that face each other across the River Thames. After a cricket match between Essex and Kent in 1776, a riot ensued. An Essex man was shot dead at the fort by men from Kent who had grabbed a gun from inside. The sergeant in command of the fort at the time was also shot dead before the men from Kent fled back across the river.

Although the docks were to come to Tilbury during the late eighteenth century, there were barges arriving at Tilbury from Kent carrying chalk long before this. Farming methods had begun to change and fields were often treated with chalk to improve the condition of the soil. This led to large numbers of chalk wagons leaving Tilbury to carry their loads throughout Essex.

As the fort was the largest building in the area, it was also used for local official business. In 1776, an inquiry was held there by the coroner on a man named William Dunnet, who was found dead in a ditch. The coroner found that he had been very much in liquor the evening before his death and had probably suffocated due to this, and had also succumbed to the bad weather.

The size of West Tilbury village hadn't increased much by the early eighteenth century. In 1723 there were only seventeen families living there. By the beginning of the nineteenth century this had increased to 104 families. The increase had a lot

The fort at Tilbury was a more imposing-looking building by the nineteenth century, as this old print shows.

to do with the arrival of the military during the war. Because many rural labourers enlisted in the army, and increased farm production was needed to feed the troops, wages in Essex rose on both farms and market gardens. This led to movement into the county by men from less affluent areas.

There was a surprise visitor to Tilbury in the late nineteenth century that showed how alliances between powers could change. The Japanese battleship, *Fuji*, spent some time at Tilbury dock in 1897. The ship was built at the Thames Ironworks and Shipbuilding Company. It was described in the *Sketch* of 5 May 1897 as a most perfect example of a modern fighting ship. The Japanese authorities were so happy that they signed a contract with the Ironworks to build another ship larger than any other battleship in existence. The ship was opened to the public, which allowed locals to inspect the powerful guns and modern design of the new naval ships of the era.

The crew of 700 men were described as strong but small. Interestingly, the report went on to say that the *Fuji* would be a match for any two ships already in the North Pacific, and even Russia's fine armoured cruisers would not expect to come off best against her. This was a statement that was to be tested within a few years during the Russo-Japanese War of 1904/5.

Above: The Japanese warship *Fuji* was built at Thames Ironworks and was one of the most modern ships afloat in 1897 when it was moored at Tilbury Docks.

Left: The *Fuji* was opened to the public while at Tilbury, giving people the opportunity to see what a modern battleship was like.

An early view of the powder mills at Waltham Abbey. The river in the foreground was used as a means of transport for barges carrying the powder to other sites such as Purfleet.

WALTHAM ABBEY

Gunpowder was first produced at Waltham Abbey in the 1660s. The site had previously been an oil mill and, under the ownership of the Walton family, became a major site. It was taken over by the government in 1787 on the advice of Sir William Congrieve, the father of the rocket maker, at a cost of £10,000.

Congrieve the younger later became controller of the laboratory at Woolwich and the mill at Waltham Abbey. He continued to update machinery and improve quality. This was due to increased demand during the French wars. The mill produced over 20,000 barrels of gunpowder in 1813. Although improvements continued after the Battle of Waterloo, the number of workers declined and production was cut to around 1,000 barrels a year.

Civil markets also became important, but the next big conflict in the Crimea led to further expansion. The use of gunpowder was later replaced in many cases by gun cotton and later cordite. The developments in explosives led to a new site south of the town, while the original site north of Waltham Abbey continued to produce gunpowder.

WARLEY

Brentwood was a market town from a very early age. It grew around the crossroads of the London to Colchester road and the Tilbury road. Warley was close to the town but its success was due to other reasons. Although sparsely populated it became a well-known horse racing area and later a famous military barracks site.

Before the war, sport was taken seriously by the army, as this point-to-point by the 8th King's Royal Irish Hussars shows. The leading horse jumping the fence is marked Self on First Attempt but is not named in the program. The second horse, Lady Timothy, is ridden by Mr H.F. Partridge.

This photograph shows Sunshine leading, ridden by Mr J.H. Charters, followed by How's That, ridden by Mr W. Cairnes.

These Steeplechases are subject to National Hunt Rules 5 and 164 to 168 as to fraudulent practices.

8th King's Royal Irish Hussars
Point=to=Point Steeplechases.

Stewards :

Brig.-Gen. E. H. ALLENBY, C.B.
Brig.-Gen. ROBB, M.V.O., C.B.
Lieut.-Colonel H. N. THOYTS.
A. SOWLER, ESQ., M.F.H.
Lieut.-Colonel H. J. LERMITTE.
Major E. DEACON.

Judge :
Col. C. BORTON, C. B.

Starter :
Sir CLAUDE de CRESPIGNY, Bart.

Clerk of Scales :
R. C. TAYLER, ESQ.

Price : SIXPENCE.

Benham and Co., 24, High Street, Colchester.

The race day programme showed that riders were a mix of military and civilian competitors.

The Married Quarters, Warley Barracks, near Brentwood.

A MERRY CHRISTMAS TO YOU

Married quarters were rare in army barracks until late in the nineteenth century. The number of children here would suggest that these married quarters at Warley were well used.

The lack of permanent barracks in England before the Napoleonic Wars was mainly due to public opposition to standing armies. There was always suspicion that an army separate from the civilian population were in danger of being misled by commanders who had ulterior motives. The first barracks in Britain were built during the eighteenth century in Ireland and Scotland where secure bases were needed for what was essentially an army of occupation.

Recruits for the army came mainly from the rural labouring class and were often enlisted by recruiting parties sent out by individual regiments. Enlisting was known as taking the King's Shilling, but in fact a much higher bounty was usually offered to recruits, plus plenty of alcohol. Unfortunately for the new recruits, most of the bounty for signing on quickly disappeared with charges for equipment – which they had to pay for themselves.

Another source of recruitment was through the law courts. The accused would often be given a choice of enlisting in the army or going to prison. It was not a recruiting method that did much to improve the standing of the army among the public.

Before barracks were built on the site, there were regular summer camps for the military at Warley. There was a royal visit in 1778 when George III and Queen Charlotte came to see the camp. This was followed by a reception for both officers from the camp and members of the local gentry. This was not unusual at Warley, as

The Essex Regiment at the Tower of London in 1885.

balls were regularly held there in a large tent. Officers in the army at this time were almost entirely from the higher echelons of society and those stationed at Warley were no different. It would have therefore been unusual if the officers had not carried on their privileged lifestyle, despite living in a tented camp.

Samuel Johnson commented on this fact after his visit. He noticed that the quality of the officer's quarters far surpassed that of the enlisted men. The officers were also active in the pursuits of the local gentry. Some officers came from the richest and most influential families in the land and would have been strongly pursued by those locals interested in mixing with such nobility.

One event that officers from the camp were involved in was the local theatre. This was actually situated in a local inn, the Lion and Lamb at Brentwood. *The Beggar's Opera* was performed under the patronage of the officers from Warley Camp, and the role of Polly Peacham in the play was played by a Mr Church. Later, officers from the Huntingdon Regiment based at the camp took part in a version of *The Mountaineer.* Amateur dramatics was a popular hobby of the rich.

Because of the situation in France and the size of the French army, there was a danger of invasion all year round, not just in the summer. Camps like Warley were therefore not enough to protect the country. There was also another point of view

The Essex Regiment at the Tower of London, 1885. The feint background may be because of either mist or poor photography.

Sergeants of the Essex Regiment at the Tower of London in August 1885. Back row, left to right: Clodd, Larret, Young, Jackes, Speek, Cullen, Lowe, Garret, Wild, Shipton. Middle row: Piper, Cann, Havers, Collet, Fibran, Clapton, Perry, Bryce, Curley, Campbell. Front row: Loach, Savage, Reeves, Freeman, Kelly, Morley, Markham, Edwards.

and that was that soldiers billeted in inns, common at the time during the winter, were close to the temptations of civilian life, something that could be restricted in army barracks.

The number of men in the army grew because of the war. In 1789 it numbered 40,000, but by 1814 it had reached 225,000. In 1793, a Barrack Department was set up by the government which became responsible for the development of army camps. The Ordnance Board dealt with artillery defences such as forts, which were also likely to have attached barracks.

The men at Warley were not just from local regiments. In June 1796 the West Yorkshire Militia arrived at the camp to spend the summer there.

The increasing fear of invasion by the armies of Napoleon led to the camp becoming a permanent fixture in 1804. A regular force of soldiers at Warley would be a support to many of the other permanent and temporary barracks set up in Essex at the time. One hundred and sixteen acres of land was purchased from the owner of Warley Manor, and the tents were replaced with buildings. Warley House was built the following year. It was a large building on the corner of Eagle Way and Warley Road and was used as quarters by the commandant of the camp.

An Act of Parliament was passed in 1806 to pay compensation to the owners of land to be used by His Majesty's Ordnance at Warley Common. There was an

The officers of the Essex Regiment, again thought to be at the Tower of London in 1885, although the background is far less imposing.

inquest at the White Hart Inn in Brentwood on 22 October 1805 – with a jury – where witnesses were examined to find out the actual value of the land to be used. Interestingly, the Act stated that if the owners were infants, lunatics or persons beyond the sea then the commissioners would decide the value.

Many of the men from the camp fought Napoleon across Europe, including the final battle at Waterloo. The end of the war brought a new problem to the area as the parish became responsible for widows of the men who died and the wounded who survived but could no longer work.

With no war to supply men, Warley, along with other barracks, became of less use. During the post-war period, the East India Company expanded their operations across the world. In 1843 the company purchased Warley Barracks for £15,000, mainly because the camp had a hospital and was bigger than their old barracks site. At first the company had traded without becoming involved in the politics in India, but when the Mughal Empire started to break up in the eighteenth century, the company began to play a part in the wars between the small states that developed.

The origins of the East India Company army were quite modest. It was expected that the force would be no more than guards for company depots and factories. It was never expected to grow into such a large force, and when it did, it caused several problems among the highest levels of British society. The company army grew from around 20,000 in the mid-eighteenth century to 150,000 by the early nineteenth century.

George III did not like the idea of a private army that was not under government control and wanted it to be amalgamated into the regular army. In the second half of the eighteenth century there were numerous attempts by politicians to achieve this, all resisted by the company. The disputes only ended when the war with France took precedence over India at the end of the century.

In 1844, a young man named Mark Crummie tried to join the 4th Dragoons. He wanted to join the cavalry so he could wear a blue coat, not a red one. He went with a friend to the Rendezvous in Westminster to enlist, but was told by a Sergeant Major that the Dragoons were no longer enlisting. Instead, he was offered the chance to join the East India Company Flying Horse, who also wore blue coats.

He was given a shilling and went to the recruitment depot at Soho Square, where a magistrate swore him in. He was then given 7s 6d and another half crown once passed by the doctor. A £4 bounty was payable when he reached Warley.

Crummie travelled to Brentwood by train with the other recruits. They disembarked the train at Brentwood and stopped at the Station Hotel for a drink before marching to Warley Common. On the way they passed another pub called the Soldier's Hope. It had a life-size picture of an artilleryman on a signboard outside and was run by a former soldier, ex-Sergeant Major James, who had served in the Bombay Foot Artillery.

Warley Barracks came as a bit of a shock to the recruits. The civilian clothes they wore were taken away and sold by auction. There was less chance of desertions if the soldiers had to run away in uniform. Most of the sergeants at the camp were pensioners from the regular army.

A carefully posed photograph of a soldier from the studio of P. Rayner at Newport Place, Warley.

There was a hospital at the camp in what had once been a row of cottages, but a new hospital was under construction. Crummie thought the food was very good. Although the men spent much of the day drilling or in working parties, in the evening most would go into Brentwood and visit the pubs.

The name Warley became well known throughout India through an unusual item. All recruits were given a chest to keep their belongings in. It became known as a Warley Box in the subcontinent. It was not very secure, however, as all the locks and keys were the same.

Officers in the East India Company army were recruited by a cadet system and arrived untrained in India. A college opened for cadets in 1804 but it was short lived. The company wanted an officer training depot in England, but were only able to operate a base on the Isle of Wight, which continued well into the nineteenth century.

As with the regular army, the number of soldiers at the barracks provided local businessmen with another set of customers. In 1844, a tender was put forward by Thomas Stone of Heron Gate offering to supply the barracks with 56,000lbs of straw for 2s 7d per hundredweight. The barracks provided custom for many local companies and dealers such as a Mr Peter Asplin of West Tilbury, who sold 400 tons of coal to the barracks at 28s a ton.

Another difference between the regular army and the East India Company was that the local parish wanted them to contribute to the rates for the local poor law. It seems that the company were against this, as a letter from Brentwood was sent to the Poor Law Commissioners at Somerset House in 1843 requesting clarification on the matter. The commissioners wrote back saying that they had no knowledge of any exemptions allotted to property owned by the East India Company.

The treatment of men in the company forces was very similar to that of the regular army. In 1844, four soldiers from Warley awaiting court martial were sent to Chelmsford Prison. Complaints by the local justices about the military using the already overcrowded prison led to their transfer to Colchester.

The East India Company may have been in possession of Warley at that time but the regiment later to become inhabitants of the barracks was also in the company area of operations, in Afghanistan. Thomas Souter was a lieutenant in the Essex Regiment and was one of a force made up of British, Indian and Afghan troops who restored a local ruler to his throne after an uprising. Then, the son of the rebel who had deposed the ruler, raised a large force but promised to let the British force and their allies leave unmolested. It was a trick and around 16,000 soldiers and camp followers were massacred. Lieutenant Souter was one of only eighty men who survived. Souter had wrapped the regiment's colours round his waist to keep it safe. In a final stand with his small group, the Afghans saw the flag and thought someone wearing such grand clothes must be very important. He became friendly with his captors and was allowed to keep the flag, which he still had when a relief column arrived and freed him. The colours were brought home and eventually hung in the regimental church at Warley.

The company also owned extensive property in the London Docklands, part of it is still known as the East India Dock. It was a necessary addition as their fleet of ships grew into a navy. One of their ships was actually named *Warley* after the barracks.

The Warley site was updated during the period that it was in the possession of the company, including the building of a church and married men's quarters. The company also had barracks at various times in Newport, Isle of Wight, Chatham in Kent and a military seminary near Croydon. The Indian Mutiny led to a wave of patriotic feeling in the area and there was a rush to enlist in the company's army.

Over the next few years thousands of recruits went through Warley and out to India. A Calvary barracks was also added to the site to reinforce the infantry and artillery already there.

Despite the improvements to the barracks, there was still not enough room for all the men they needed. This led to the billeting of men among the local population in both private houses and inns, providing a welcome source of income for the less well-off locals.

The situation had changed concerning the company after 1833 when an Act of Parliament renewed the company charter for £630,000 a year. The company then ran two-thirds of India as agents for the government. Indian princes were responsible for the other third.

After the Indian Mutiny the government took over the administration of India and began to send regular troops to the country so there was no longer any need for the East India Company to have their own forces. In 1860 therefore the government bought Warley back from the company. It became the home of the 44th and 56th Regiments of Foot who became the Essex Regiment.

WEELEY

In 1814, the barrack master at Weeley, William Goddard, obtained a similar position in barracks in Gibraltar. However, following a robbery at Weeley Barracks, Goddard was forced to put off taking up his new position to act as a witness at the trial. It was discovered that tiles had been removed from a storeroom at the barracks and a large quantity of old sheeting had been stolen. The weight of the cloth was over six hundredweight. A man named Charles Bickers had been seen speaking to some soldiers at the storehouse shortly before the theft. A search was carried out at Bickers' house and a large amount of the stolen material was found.

The Commissioner for the Affairs of Barracks sent a letter to Weeley in February instructing them to employ a professional gentleman in the area to prosecute

The garrison from the Martello towers, such as this one just visible in the distance at Walton-on-the-Naze, were based at Weeley due to the unhealthy air in coastal regions.

Although Weeley Barracks were long gone when this photograph was taken, the tower still seemed to be in use as the flag shows.

Bickers. The letter advised that the person responsible for prosecuting him should contact the Revd Mr Jefferson of Weeley, an intelligent magistrate who had taken an active part in the investigation.

The Acting Barrack Master, John Read, had by then taken over from Goddard. He stated that Bickers claimed to have bought the sheeting from a soldier named Farran. The soldier Farran, however, was an Irishman of the 30th Regiment who had been a prisoner of war in France. He denied all knowledge of the matter. A statement from the Revd Jefferson stated that Bickers was a bad character.

From the reports, it seems that Bickers' guilt was as good as decided, so William Goddard was allowed to take up his new position in Gibraltar and not appear as a witness. Unfortunately, the sentence Bickers received is unknown.

Soldiers at the time of the French wars were often involved in dealing with smugglers as well as the enemy. While at Weeley in 1814, members of the 55th Regiment were alerted to a man acting suspiciously by Mrs Shirley, the wife of the naval lieutenant in charge of Holland Signal Station. The soldiers found a number of smuggled containers of spirits. These were taken to Harwich where it was then found that many of the containers were missing, supposedly stolen by the soldiers.

Weeley Barracks closed shortly after the end of the war with Napoleon. The demise of the barracks left the village much as it was before the troops arrived. In White's *History, Gazetteer & Directory of Essex 1848*, Weeley was described as a pleasant village on mainly one street with about 700 residents. Today, there is nothing left in the area to commemorate the barracks apart from the gravestones of a few soldiers in the cemetery.

YEOMANRY

The connection of men with the military was much greater in the past than the present day. The village greens of many Essex towns and villages were often the scene of training and meetings of local volunteer units. The militia had a long history in Essex as well as in other parts of the country.

During the 1850s, the formation of the rifle corps had replaced the militia, and at the time there were some calls to disband the Yeomanry. This was decided against, but changes were put in place. Unmounted riflemen were attached to mounted Yeomanry groups and were carried in carts.

The skill shown by the Yeomanry Artillery on Wanstead Flats impressed the watching crowd.

In June 1853, over 200 members of the West Essex Yeomanry assembled on Wanstead Flats. They trained for eight days and were commanded by Major Palmer. They were divided into four troops, including artillery. A Troop was commanded by Captain Jessop of Waltham Abbey. B Troop were mainly recruited from the Harlow area and was commanded by Captain Watlington. C Troop was commanded by the Honourable F. Petre, and the artillery by Captain Edenborough.

A large crowd of spectators was drawn by the band, which led the men to where they were inspected by the Honourable Major Pitt of the Royal Horse Guards. This was followed by a display of military manoeuvres. One of these involved firing the guns, and before the smoke had cleared, the guns were completely dismantled.

Sir Arundell Neave Bart was a captain in the 3rd Essex Dragoons from 1829. He was obviously well travelled, as demonstrated by this photograph (above) taken in Naples.

The day ended with a large gathering, which included over 300 guests drawn from the local nobility. This took place in a tent erected on the site where the palatial Wanstead House had once stood.

Despite the obvious skill demonstrated by the artillery on Wanstead Flats, their days were numbered. By the 1870s it was decided that artillery and unmounted troops were no longer to be part of the Yeomanry. Instead, they were to become solely light cavalry units.

FOUR

The Twentieth Century to the First World War

T he early twentieth century was the heyday of the part-time Yeomanry groups. Weekend and summer camps were organised where mounted soldiers from all parts of the county would converge for mock battles and training. Weekend fêtes on village greens were not complete without a display of the skills of these mounted part-time warriors.

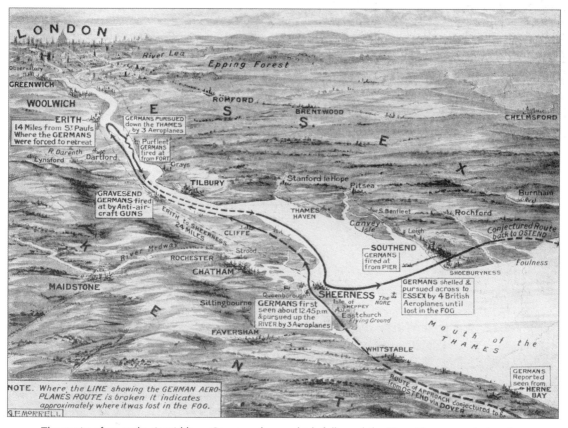

The route of an early air raid by a German plane, which followed the River Thames up to London.

HMS *Essex* was launched in 1901. It was a Monmouth class and the only armoured cruiser with three funnels.

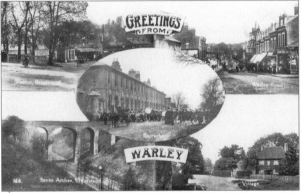

The ESSEX are with the rest
For King and Country they'll do their best !

Above: A sign of the times. This early postcard has Warley barracks as its central view.

Left: A patriotic card showing that the Essex Regiment were going to play their part in the war.

When the First World War began, the county became the site of numerous military camps much as it had been during the Napoleonic Wars, but on a much greater scale. Every spare piece of land became the home of part of Kitchener's civilian army. The training many of these men received was at best sparse, and they soon found themselves up to their knees in mud in foreign trenches before their patriotic enthusiasm began to wane. For the first time a foreign war also began to be visited on the home front with air raids from Zeppelins and later from aircraft.

BARKING

An eighteen-year-old man from Abbey Road, Barking, was awarded the Victoria Cross for his bravery during the Battle of Le Cateau. Job Henry Drain was a driver for the Royal Horse Artillery 37th Battery. He had joined the army two years previously and had been stationed in Ireland before being part of the first British Expeditionary Force. At Le Cateau, Drain was one of a group who volunteered to save some guns with the enemy only 100yds away.

Drain's old headmaster at Back Lane Church of England School remembered him as one of the worst boys in the school – always playing truant and up to mischief. He had in fact completed his schooling at Walthamstow Truant School. Drain's parents claimed their son had only played truant because he would rather have been at work. Strangely, it was the school attendance officer who knocked on their door to tell them of their son's award.

When Drain returned home, he was given a complimentary dinner at the council offices in Barking by Councillor A.E. Martin. Also attending were W. Thorne, a local MP, the Bishop of Barking and H. Dyer, the Mayor of West Ham. Mayor Dyer actually arranged a commission for Drain in the Artillery Brigade, which he was happy to accept.

The Essex Regiment spent time in several parts of the country. This is a camp in Worthing.

Camp Life at CHELMSFORD --- I don't think !

A humorous card showing the easy life at Chelmsford Camp. These types of cards were produced for a number of camps during the First World War.

CHELMSFORD

Although the employment of women in factories had been a common event during the beginnings of the industrial revolution, the outbreak of war turned back the clock as the men went off to fight and the munitions factories became dependant on female workers.

Chelmsford was one of the first towns in the county to open a hostel for female munitions workers. The hostel provided cheap meals for the residents. There was also a rest room supplied with reading material where Bible classes were held on a Sunday.

Although originally for munitions workers, the hostel was opened on market days for the increased number of women who took over jobs on the land and who came into the town on those days. This was one of the first hostels for land workers in the country.

The hostel also ran an evening club for the girls where there would be singing and dancing. On one evening a week a male friend could accompany the girls to the club – very progressive for the time. As well as factory girls, the town was also the base of recruits in the new civilian army. Many recruits for the Essex Regiment arrived from other parts of the county and found Chelmsford Drill Hall occupied by Boer War veteran Corporal Bloggs, who would send them on their way to their billets, usually with a local family who were paid 3*s* 4*d* a week for their new guest.

There were a number of different regiments based in Chelmsford during the war. This is a member of the Gloucestershire Regiment and was taken in the town.

Below: The racecourse at Galleywood was used as barracks for troops during the war, but was used for racing again when peace returned.

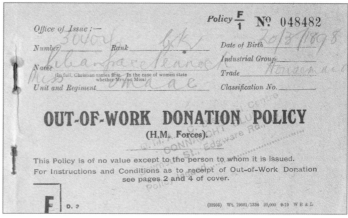

The end of the war led to high numbers of unemployed ex-soldiers. This is an example of an out-of-work donation policy. It paid 29s a week to ex-soldiers who found themselves unemployed.

The recruits often spent their mornings running around the town, which seemed to be the only training they got at first, and this was mostly carried out in civilian clothes. They would then spend the evenings in the local pubs. They were eventually provided with ill-fitting uniforms. The officers in charge of these men were mainly Essex gentlemen, most fresh from public schools.

The Army used Clacton as a practice site for landing an invasion force, which included horses.
This old print from 1904 shows that it was not without problems.

CLACTON

Many areas of the Essex coast have been used for invasion practice throughout history. In 1904 it was Clacton's turn. Artillery was brought ashore and was taken along the beaches. The event was a welcome entertainment for the holidaymakers still in the town as the summer drew to a close. It was also watched by a number of VIPs.

There was another visit by an important person in 1914, but this one was unplanned. Winston Churchill, then First Lord of the Admiralty, was travelling by aeroplane from Felixstowe when the aircraft was forced to make an emergency landing at Clacton. While waiting for a replacement plane he was verbally abused by suffragettes.

One of the worries when the war broke out was that the town would be attacked by German ships. The old Martello towers from the Napoleonic Wars were called back into use as billets for soldiers posted to Clacton.

Some of the horses obviously did make it ashore.

The police seemed to take an interest when guns were landed on the beach as well.

COLCHESTER

As well as being the site of several barracks, Colchester was also the victim of bombing by Zeppelin during the First World War. Propaganda was an important weapon during the conflict and so the cowardly air attacks were described as being carried out by 'Sky Pirates' and 'Baby Killers' in the *Daily Mirror* of 23 February 1915. One headline claimed that the Germans had failed to kill one baby and even showed photographs of a bombed house. The house was the home of a Quartermaster Sergeant Radjohn, and it was his baby who had been in the house that the raiders had failed to kill.

The Zeppelin arrived on the Sunday night and dropped firebombs on Colchester and Braintree. The Radjohns' baby's pram was blown out of the shed and the rear of the house badly damaged, but thankfully the baby was asleep in the front of the house and escaped injury.

There were some parts of Essex where it was possible to see many of the German attacks by both plane and Zeppelin. Chignal St James was in the centre of the county but was often overflown by enemy aircraft. It was also the site of a temporary airfield that was lit up during heavy raids to give unreliable planes that were fighting the Germans an emergency landing spot. In September 1916, the field was bombed by a Zeppelin whose crew obviously thought the lights were part of something important.

Everyone in the town wanted to show how their menfolk were ready to do their duty, as this card shows.

We Terriers get some
Strange Views into our   COLCHESTER
Heads at

A novelty card, which must have given the families of men posted to the town some idea of where their loved ones were. The hat lifted up to reveal a folded series of views of the town.

Also visible from Chignal St James was the shooting down of the Zeppelin L32 by Lieutenant Sowery from Hornchurch airfield. It was also possible to hear the cheers of thousands of soldiers from the camps in Colchester applauding the event. But the excitement was not over, as another Zeppelin was brought down within minutes of the first – this one crashing in the direction of Maldon. By morning, the area around Billericay, where the first Zeppelin had been brought down by Lieutenant Sowery, was packed with people. Soldiers keeping the crowd back surrounded the site, and a British airship circled overhead.

The German crew of about twenty all perished. Their bodies, dressed in thick clothes and their boots covered with thick felt slippers, were placed in a nearby barn. The doors of the barn were broken open the following night by someone who obviously wanted to have a closer look. The crew were buried in one large grave in Great Burstead churchyard, but the commander was given a separate burial.

The second Zeppelin had attempted to get back to Germany but was obviously too badly damaged and had turned back and landed at Little Wigborough. The crew survived the landing and, after burning their ship, threw away their guns. While looking for some soldiers to surrender to they were arrested by some policemen who happened along. They spent the night in the church hall at Mersea and were taken to Colchester in the morning.

A band leading the troops at Soberon Barracks. There were several barracks in the town, most dating from years before the war.

Firing practice at the artillery barracks. The noise must have rivalled the sound of the large guns in France that could be heard in many parts of Essex.

Colchester was the victim of air raids by Zeppelins, which caused much damage.

The year 1916 was the last to see a real threat from Zeppelins. They had by then become too vulnerable from attack, despite seeming invincible before this. They were replaced with the increased use of aeroplanes, and so began the dogfight above the skies of Essex.

As well as an increase in the number of soldiers to the town there was also an influx of female munitions workers who came from other parts of the country. A Girls' Patriotic Club opened in the town, providing a place for girls, now living in a strange town, to meet others in the same position in a social atmosphere. Unusually, the club was also open to soldiers, who also found themselves in strange new surroundings.

DAGENHAM

Although Dagenham was still a small village at the time of the First World War, it did play a role in arming the country. This was mainly due to the docks that had been built on the Dagenham bank of the Thames at the end of the nineteenth century. There was an old rail link to the Dagenham marshes, which dated back to the Franco-Prussian War when an Ordnance depot had been established in the area for a short period. This old track was joined to the new dock area establishing transport links.

It was due to the growth of the docks that the last great ship built on the Thames was to arrive at Dagenham in 1911. The Thames had been a centre of shipbuilding in the past when the oak trees that grew in Essex were used, but once ships began to be built from iron the centre of production moved northwards. By 1910, Thames Ironworks was the only shipbuilding yard left on the river. One of their most famous ships, the *Thunderer*, built in 1910, turned out to be the last from the same yard that had built the first British ironclad in 1860, the *Warrior*. The ironworks may have left the world of shipbuilding, but they left something else behind: a football team that evolved into West Ham United.

Everyone in the country was thinking of the men serving overseas, especially when the terrible conditions in the trenches became known.

The call on the terraces of 'come on you irons' and the crossed hammers on their club badge is an indication of its origins.

Because of her size, there was nowhere on the upper Thames where the *Thunderer* could berth, so she was fitted out at Dagenham Dock. The ship was later towed downriver by seven tugs. The *Thunderer* was completed in 1912, but had a short lifespan after being sunk with all hands at the Battle of Jutland in 1916.

The dock at Dagenham saw more use at the end of the war, when army equipment brought back from France was landed there. The primitive track to the site of the docks was rebuilt to become Chequers Lane.

DUNMOW

Dunmow may have been a small place, but it played an important part in the conflicts that affected Essex.

A Private Gibson of the Grenadier Guards had been much decorated during the Boer War. When he died in 1914, he was the first soldier to be given military honours at a funeral in the town. Gibson's funeral was held in the same year that conflict again came to the country. That summer, a notice was placed in the post office window informing the town's inhabitants that the country was at war. In those days of restricted contact in rural areas, it is no doubt true that many of those living in remote areas would have been unaware of the outbreak of war until some time after it began.

Digging trenches was part of the training for many regiments before they went abroad. The Essex Regiment are seen here digging trenches 'somewhere in England'.

A plaque commemorating Jack
Cornwell, who won a posthumous
Victoria Cross at the Battle of
Jutland at the age of sixteen.

The sound of gunfire from the war in Europe could be heard in the town. There was an evacuation plan in place in the event of invasion: women and children were to be carried away by horse and cart.

Over 200 men returned from the war to attend a celebration dinner. The men from the town who did not return were commemorated in 1921 when the war memorial was unveiled.

Colonel Thomas Gibbons was a well-known figure in Dunmow and had military experience as a captain in the Essex Volunteer Regiment. They became the 5th Essex Territorials, and were sent to the ill-fated landing at Gallipoli. Although wounded, Colonel Gibbons took charge of the regiment. He was wounded twice more in Palestine after the regiment was sent to the Middle East.

HARWICH

Harwich played an unusual part in the beginning of the First World War. When war was declared, German Embassy staff travelled by train from Liverpool Street station to the town, before being taken across to Holland on one of the steamers. The Harwich boats were later to carry refugees back to Britain in the opposite direction. The ferries continued to cross to the continent despite the threat from German U-boats.

No 12

Le S S. Brussels coulé à l'extrémité du Môle et son héroïque capitaine Fryatt capturé le 23 juin 1916 et fusillé à Bruges le 27 juillet 1916.

The S. S. "Brussels" sunk near the extremity of Zeebrugge-Mole, and her heroic Captain Fryatt, who was captured on the 23rd June 1916 and shot on the 27th July 1916.

Het stoomschip Brussels gezonken op het uiteinde van de Pier en zijn heldhaftigen kapitein Fryatt, gevangen genomen den 23en Juni 1916 en doodgeschoten te Brugge den 27en Juli 1916.

Above: Captain Fryatt, of the steamship *Brussels*, rammed a German U-boat while crossing to the continent from Harwich. On a later trip he was taken prisoner and shot.

Left: Technology was still not in an advanced state during the war, as these Essex cycle scouts show.

The port became the home of the Harwich Force, whose task was to keep the shipping lanes open. Despite being closed to visitors – one of the only restricted areas during the war – one person was allowed in: the late Queen Mother, who arrived in the town to stay with her sister.

The redoubt was used for a number of purposes during the war, and at one point in 1918 a young lieutenant, Ewing, returned wounded from France and was put in command of the defence. At the time there were around a hundred men stationed there. For a time the moat was used to breed rabbits to supplement the food supply. Unfortunately, a disease struck the enterprise and the rabbit breeding came to an end.

The end of the war was a typically British affair. When the fleet of defeated German U-boats sailed into Harwich, Admiral Tyrwhitt ordered that no celebrations were to be seen by the defeated Germans.

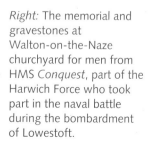

Above: The guns at Beacon Hill Fort were manned by the men of the Essex and Suffolk Royal Garrison Artillery.

Right: The memorial and gravestones at Walton-on-the-Naze churchyard for men from HMS *Conquest*, part of the Harwich Force who took part in the naval battle during the bombardment of Lowestoft.

The Kynochtown Hotel, which was built close to the munitions factory.

KYNOCHTOWN

The explosives factory of Kynoch & Co. began its life in Essex at the end of the nineteenth century. The company was preparing to increase production for the Boer War and already had factories in other parts of the country. They bought Borley Farm at Shell Haven, close to Canvey Island. The site was not the easiest to build on as it was in the marshy land alongside the river.

Along with rifle bullets, a variety of explosives were made at the factory. Most of the buildings were set apart from each other for safety in case there was an explosion, which would then be restricted to one place.

The site was situated in a remote position, which caused problems for the workforce who had difficulty getting there. The only form of transport available at the time was horse and cart. To counter this problem, the company built houses for the workers. They also added a school and a shop, and Kynochtown began its life. Just after the town was built a light railway line was laid from Corringham, which solved the transport problem.

The First World War led to a great expansion in the output of the factory and included an increase in the number of women employed. The complex was guarded by the military and was fenced off to keep out any suspicious characters. This did little to protect against air raids however.

There was an interesting idea put forward about the factory by a member of the Sportsman's Battalion, which was based at Hornchurch. The sportsmen had been digging trenches at Leigh-on-Sea in 1915 for coastal defences, and when the area

Above: When the village by the factory was taken over and renamed Coryton, the station was also renamed.

Right: The munitions works were the target of several air raids when bombs including incendiaries such as this one found at Maldon, were dropped.

GERMAN INCENDIARY BOMB. WEIGHT ABOUT 16 lbs. DROPPED AT MALDON DURING AIR RAID. APRIL 16.15.

was bombed, John Chessire wrote in a letter to his wife saying that the Zeppelins were probably aiming for the explosives factory. He suggested that German prisoners be held at the site to deter the bombers or at least to punish their own countrymen.

There was expansion of the site during the war and huts were built to house the increased number of workers. There was also a company hospital, quite an enlightened move for an employer at the time.

The factory closed shortly after the war as there was less need for explosives, and the factory had been in an exposed position which made it liable to air attack. In the early 1920s the site was bought by Cory Brothers Ltd, who turned it into an oil refinery. The village was renamed Coryton.

ANYTHING YOU DON'T SEE ASK FOR

Camp Life at PURFLEET --- I don't think !

Another example of a humorous card showing the easy life of men at Purfleet Camp.

PURFLEET

There were several problems at Purfleet during the war years. One was related to the health of the men at the camp. The dust shoot at nearby Rainham, which was used to dump rubbish, attracted so many flies to the area that there were moves to close it for the benefit of the camp's inmates.

There were also several more individual problems relating to health and safety. Private Stephen Tracy, of the 15th Battalion Royal Fusiliers, was knocked down by a train and killed while stationed at Purfleet. Private Tracy, who was from Lancashire, was hit by a train while crossing the railway lines at Aveley on his way back to camp. He was killed instantly.

In September 1915, a cutter from the training ship, the *Cornwall*, moored at Purfleet, was hit by a government tug. The cutter contained one officer and twenty-six boys aged between thirteen and eighteen. The officer and sixteen boys drowned. The officer, Fred Lane, was an ex-Naval petty officer. Several boats were launched from both the *Cornwall* and the shore, and ten of the cutter's occupants were saved.

At an inquest held at the Royal Hotel, Samuel Robinson, the schoolmaster on board the *Cornwall*, identified the bodies. The commander of the ship, Captain Steele, also attended the inquest. The commander of the tug, William Blackmore, was a company sergeant major of the Royal Engineers based at Dover. He was a master mariner by trade and said that the cutter had changed direction and cut across in front of the tug.

The Knuts of Purfleet Huts: a group of fusiliers at the camp. The first soldier on the left in the front row looks much younger than the rest.

The Royal Hotel at Purfleet was popular with the upper classes, who travelled down from London by boat to spend evenings at the hotel.

ROMFORD

Numerous soldiers were based in Romford and the surrounding area during the war. There were also attempts to involve local people in preparations for the conflict. A rifle range was opened at the rear of the Picture Pavilion cinema in South Street. The cost of membership was half a crown per annum and *2d* per visit, which included the use of a rifle and ten rounds of ammunition.

One of the units based in the town was the B Battery, 271st Brigade Royal Field Artillery. Two members of the unit, Edwin Blackwell and Edwin Axe, recorded their wartime experiences in a book called *Romford to Beirut*. The journey took them some time, for, after leaving Romford in August 1915, they spent three years in France and time in Egypt before they finally reached their destination.

They obviously did not spend all their time fighting in Syria, as their book details a touching story of their time in the town of Hadeth. One day, a young girl of around two years of age wandered into the store shed. Quartermaster Sergeant Bryant and a few other men nominated themselves as temporary mother. The child made remarkable progress from its malnourished condition, and when they left the town, bound for Egypt in December 1918, Major Martin and the other officers found the girl a place in a mission.

Perhaps one of the best-remembered units to come to Romford was the 2nd Sportsman's Battalion, who were stationed at Hare Hall Camp. The 1st Battalion were also nearby at Grey Towers camp in Hornchurch.

The 2nd Battalion arrived at Hare Hall Camp on 17 March 1915. The camp was similar to that at Grey Towers but had some modifications, including showers. One

Camp life at Romford with the Sportsman's Battalion.

recruit with local connections was Sir Herbert Raphael, a former inhabitant of Gidea Hall who was instrumental in developing the Gidea Park Housing Estate. Sir Herbert was MP for South Derbyshire at the time.

Sir Herbert's membership of the battalion was raised in Parliament when it was reported that Lady Raphael was in receipt of a War Separation Allowance of 16s a week. It raised a laugh in the House when it was stated that at least Lady Raphael would not be in financial difficulties. The money was in fact given to charity.

Another famous unit at Hare Hall Camp were the Artists Rifles, who had by that time become an officer training unit. There was a further connection between the Artists and the Sportsman's Battalion in the shape of Private W.S. Ferrie.

The Sportsman's Battalion were replaced at Hare Hall Camp by the Artists Rifles Officer Training Corps.

Private Ferrie was a minister in the United Free Church in Scotland who had tried to join the Inns of Court Officer Training Corps. Unfortunately for him they did not recognise Glasgow University, which he had attended, as one of their establishments. There was at that time a list of schools and universities which were seen as suitable backgrounds for officer candidates. Anyone who had not attended these was unlikely to be accepted for officer training. Things began to change later on, as a shortage of officers grew acute.

Ferrie joined the 2nd Sportsman's Battalion instead, and provided several insights into their time at Romford. Although the battalion was allowed to enlist men up to the age of forty-five, Ferrie claimed there was actually a man of sixty-four at Romford who had lied about his age.

Ferrie seemed to enjoy his time at Romford. He attended a football match between the 1st and 2nd Sportsman's Battalions at Romford Town's ground. He was one of the men who were allowed to visit the brewery. He would also preach in the local Congregational church in Romford to both soldiers and members of the local population.

Not everything was to his taste, however, and he mentioned how many men from the camp would go into town to make friends with the local girls. He describes the behaviour of these girls as making themselves as cheap as he had never seen such a thing anywhere but in Romford. He accused the men who associated with them as making themselves cheap as well.

Ferrie did not spend all his time enjoying himself. Much of the training of the 2nd Battalion seemed to involve digging trenches. The men would take the train in the morning into parts of Essex and dig trenches for the day. During a half-hour break for lunch, the men would often go to a local pub. Sir Herbert Raphael would usually pay for the drinks of all his company.

A number of large houses were turned into hospitals for the wounded from the trenches. From the address of the photographer, it is thought that this one was in Romford.

While at Romford, Ferrie tried to get a commission, and was finally transferred to the Argyll & Sutherland Highlanders. In December 1915 Ferrie returned to Hare Hall, but by then the Sportsman's Battalion had gone and he came back as a member of the Artist Rifles for officer training. He mentioned that the training was very good with lectures by the former Director of Sandhurst Military Academy. There were also only twenty-five men to a hut where there had been forty during the spell of the Sportsman's Battalion at the camp.

With the Artists at Romford were two of the best-remembered war poets, Edward Thomas and Wilfred Owen. Owen had arrived at Romford in November 1915. He described it as nicely set out with about forty huts in rows divided by services huts. The training was described as very hard by Owen, and included trench digging around a local crossroads, which helped to develop a military eye. Owen found the training and the camping quite difficult. He also found it difficult to mix with some of the members of the Artists who came from much more illustrious backgrounds than he did. After a trip to Romford baths, Owen claimed that only danger and nakedness could obliterate social distinction.

Owen made friends with some local boys, members of the Boy Scouts who were helping around the camp. Two of the boys, Raymond Williams and Albert Harper, lived in Emerson Park and invited Owen back to their homes. Boy Scouts were given jobs during the war, including guarding bridges and carrying messages. Raymond won a war badge for his war work.

At the beginning of 1916, the pubs and hotels in Romford were made out of bounds by the camp's commander due to drunkenness among the men. This was not a popular decision with the local population. In February, measles hit the camp and the men in many of the huts found themselves in quarantine so they could not even visit the YMCA hut on the camp.

In the spring, Owen was moved to Balgores House in Balgores Lane, where he was treated more like an officer, with meals being served to him by batmen. There was still a lot of training, which often took place on Romford golf course. In March a Zeppelin dropped bombs close to the camp before it crashed off the Kent coast. In early June Owen was discharged from the Artists and joined the Manchester Regiment.

SAFFRON WALDEN

During the First World War the male inhabitants of Saffron Walden, as with many other towns in the county, rushed to join the forces. The house that was later to become the home of the fire brigade captain was then the recruiting office for those wishing to join Kitchener's army. The man responsible for recruitment was Colour Sergeant Jarman, who had been the commissionaire at the local cinema. Jarman had served in the Boer War and earned good money at his new position – he was paid half a crown for each man he managed to recruit.

Each recruit went before the doctor, J.P. Atkinson, whose medical examinations were so thorough that he could do two per minute. He was also paid half a crown per recruit. After being passed fit, the men were sworn in by the doctor's father and the mayor who gave each of them the King's Shilling and a railway ticket to their training destination.

Gymnastics instructors from the Essex Regiment, 1916.

The Royal Naval Pageant, 1909. Ships of the Home and Atlantic Fleets gathered on the Thames off Southend.

SOUTHEND

At around 3 a.m. one morning in May 1915, a number of loud explosions woke the people of Southend. A special constable named Redhouse saw a Zeppelin hovering above the town, dropping one bomb after another. Around a hundred bombs were dropped in the raid, which lasted no more than twenty minutes.

A card from a series produced by Bell's of Westcliff showing England's warships.

The first bomb hit a house in York Road where a soldier was billeted, slightly injuring him. Another bomb embedded itself in the road at Cobweb Corner.

Most of the other bombs dropped were incendiaries, one of which led to the only fatality of the raid when it went through the roof of the home of Mr Whitwell, a council employee. He was seriously injured and his wife was killed. Fires were started in several buildings by the other bombs, and some fell on the beach. One bomb fell near a ship moored by the pier, which was being used to house 1,200 interned German civilians.

While there was large-scale naval involvement at Southend, nearby Shoeburyness had a large military presence. This shows the main entrance to the barracks at Shoeburyness.

The camp field crossing at Shoeburyness. There was a railway line running through much of the town's army camp which originated in the nineteenth century.

The coastguard station at Shoeburyness in the years before the war. The coastguard would watch river traffic on its way to Southend.

Anti-aircraft guns in the area were fired at the Zeppelin and drove it off towards London. Troops were called out to help fight the fires, especially the large blaze in Mr Flaxman's timber yard. Despite widespread damage and one death, the town had escaped lightly.

Southend airport had its origins in the First World War and it was mainly the air raids that led to its creation. It was intended to protect the country against air raids by German Gotha bombers, but by the time it opened the threat from Zeppelins had as good as disappeared. The field began with no. 61 squadron, who flew Sopwith Pups until they later exchanged these for SE5s.

TILBURY

There was some excitement at Tilbury in November 1914 when several German prisoners, who were over the age of military service, were sent home from Dorchester PoW camp. As they were being loaded aboard a lugger on their way to a ship, one of the men helping them noticed something suspicious in a large packing case. It turned out to be a German lieutenant who had escaped captivity and was trying to get back to Germany with the civilians.

Owing to the war, improvements were made to the road to Tilbury Fort from Southend Road, near the Cock Inn. The major cost of the improvements was paid for by the Road Board, leaving Orsett Rural District Council to pay an amount that was only equal to what they would have paid in the upkeep of the old road. There were then plans for a further road improvement to the highway towards Brentwood, and no doubt Warley Barracks, where a great number of troops were based. Road improvements meant that reinforcements could be quickly moved to the area if needed, and men being sent abroad from Tilbury could also travel there.

WALTHAM ABBEY

The First World War brought a previously unheard of expansion in the amount of explosives needed. Millions of shells were fired at the German trenches and each had to be supplied with explosives.

The number of workers at Waltham Abbey almost doubled during the war to more than 6,000. Most of these workers were female; male workers were in short supply due to the demands of the trenches. Work continued twenty-four hours a day and the site was again enlarged. Cordite was being produced at the rate of 140 tons per week.

Barges were still used for transporting powder away from the site and for bringing in raw materials. Small barges were used inside the mills, which had its own system of internal canals.

Photo of the 1/6th ESSEX REGIMENTAL BOOT REPAIRERS
Instructed and Equipped by

R.J. Blindell.
BOOT FACTOR

19, MARKET PLACE (OPPOSITE TOWN HALL), **ST. ALBANS.**
58b, LONDON ROAD (NEAR WATSON'S WALK).

Reliable PROMPTLY EXECUTED **R**epairs BY **M**en and **M**achinery

CONTRACTOR TO TERRITORIAL BATTALIONS
Enquiries Solicited.

Willsons', New Walk Printing Works, Leicester.

An advertisement for boot repairers from the Essex Regiment. It seems they were trained by the company named on the leaflet.

WARLEY

The 1st Battalion of the Essex Regiment had been stationed at Warley when ordered to Africa to take part in the Boer War. They arrived in Cape Town at the end of 1899 and were commanded by Colonel T.E. Stephenson. They replaced the Suffolk Regiment at Colesberg, and in February 1900 were involved in the fight with Cronje's retreating army.

They later fought at Paardeberg with the 18th Rifles Brigade, and in March 1900 at Driefontein. They suffered eighty casualties after attacking two strong positions in a bayonet charge. The regiment provided a guard of honour at Pretoria in May and fought again at Belfast in August.

In 1903, the 2nd Battalion of the Essex Regiment marched through the county to attract the attention of the local population. This was quite successful, as they managed to enlist thirty-five recruits on the way. In December that year, Sir Evelyn Ward unveiled a memorial in the Warley Garrison Chapel to the 209 men from the Essex Regiment who had died in the Boer War.

The Essex Regiment has one of the less glorious distinctions of the First World War. Although many private soldiers were executed during the conflict for various offences, only a few officers were executed. One of these was Second Lieutenant

The barracks at Warley, which was still a rural area at the time of the First World War.

The hospital at the barracks, which dated back to the time of the East India Company.

Another view of the barracks.

John Patterson of the Essex Regiment, who was found guilty not only of desertion but also of shooting a military policeman who tried to stop him.

The size of the Essex Regiment First greatly expanded during the First World War. One of the new units in the regiment were the 10th Essex Battalion. Recruits for the new battalion ended up in a tented camp at Shorncliffe, Kent, but were quickly moved to Colchester in October 1914 and found themselves in Hyderabad Barracks. The new unit was mainly consisted of men from the East End of London, Essex and even Norfolk and Suffolk.

Also in October, the 1st Battalion Essex Regiment returned to Warley after ten years abroad. A large crowd turned out to welcome them but were surprised to see the men in shorts and pith helmets, as despite it being a British autumn the battalion only possessed hot weather kit.

In November 1914, Captain Bernard Ward of the 6th Battalion the Essex Regiment married Miss Norah Viney of Leeds, at Costessey near Norwich. The captain was the son of the former commandant Colonel J. Breaker-Ward. The bridal carriage was pulled by the sergeants of the battalion, was led by a band and followed by the men of the company. Attached to the 6th Battalion at Norwich was the West Ham Division of the National Reserve. The members of this division were mainly employees of the West Ham Tramways department.

The troops at Warley Barracks had several visitors during the war, some more famous than others. One of these was Lord Kitchener, who came to inspect the Irish Guards on 15 January 1915. He had become their honorary colonel. He was presented to the troops by Lieutenant Colonel the Earl of Kerry, the guard's commanding officer. Lord Kitchener said how proud he was to command such a fine regiment.

A less famous visitor was the Bishop of Chelmsford. He spoke to a gathering of the men in the camp chapel on 5 February 1915. These included members of the Irish Guards, the Essex Regiment and the 2nd North Midland RAMC Brigade Territorials.

There were battalions in the army that accepted older men to fight in the war such as the Sportsman's Battalion of the Royal Fusiliers but in the Essex Regiment it seemed that there were no such allowances. On one of their first days in France a shell case landed close to a newly arrived unit. A man rushed out to pick it up as a souvenir and burnt his fingers on it. The next day he went sick and never came back. He was described as being aged about forty and much too old for war.

The terrible days of trench warfare were obviously yet to come for some members of the Essex Regiment. The 10th Essex arrived in Amiens in August 1915 and were the first British troops to shop in the town, where, it was reported, prices were still reasonable. The first six weeks spent by the 10th in France were mainly taken up in training and swimming races with the London Regiments attached to the fifth division. The time was described as a being like a fine outdoor holiday.

Far from being awash in seas of mud, the early trenches were clean and tidy. Every morning there would be a trench inspection by the company commander and every empty cartridge case and scrap of paper had to be picked up and disposed of. The trenches were even swept with home-made brooms.

Inside the barrack square, with a group of men.

Military Funeral leaving Warley Barracks Brentwood.

A military funeral leaving Warley Barracks. There seems to be little public interest in the event.

The running of parts of the trench depended on the commanding officer. In 1916, the colonel in charge of one trench decided that everyone should leave their rifle on the parapet of the trench in each man's firing position. The result was that eleven men sheltering in a dug out were blocked in when a shell fell by the entrance. They dug themselves out only to find a German raiding party waiting for them. They had no means of fighting as their rifles were still on the parapet and they were taken prisoner.

There was a landmark event in March 1916 when a German plane flew over the 10th Essex camp in the Somme Valley. The plane returned and attempted to bomb the camp but missed by about a mile. They were very lucky to have been missed – particularly considering there was no blackout in those days and every tent was lit up by candles.

Towards the end of the war, the 10th had lost most of the members of their band. They solved this problem by stealing a band from another regiment. The 12th Middlesex band had been surplus to requirements after a reorganisation. They were destined for the Royal Berkshires, but through a manipulation of documents they were transferred into the Essex Regiment.

In August 1918, as the end of the First World War drew near, the Americans led an attack on the Somme, accompanied by tanks. The 10th Essex followed up behind and collected a few souvenirs. In one German pack they found one of the most memorable finds of the war: the Essex Battalion flag. It had been lost in the retreat that had taken place two days earlier.

YEOMANRY

There were annual camps for the Yeomanry in the years before the First World War. In May 1912 the camp was at Harlow. Instructions in the *Essex Yeomanry Magazine* for that month instructed the Colchester, Harwich, Walton and Clacton troops to proceed by train to Harlow. The Ardleigh Troop was to march there. Southend Troop was to be billeted at Weald Hall, Brentwood, on the way, as were Orsett Troop.

At times of annual camp, the whole county must have been alive with troops of Yeomanry travelling the roads and lanes of the county on their way to camp.

Essex Yeomanry Magazine from October 1913.

The Essex Yeomanry officers, NCOs and other ranks still serving in 1913.

Essex Yeomanry officers attending training at Colchester in 1913.

The training and manoeuvres of these part-time soldiers obviously did not always go to plan. A report on Easter Monday Operations in the May *Essex Yeomanry Magazine* reported how a hostile force of London and Hertfordshire Yeomanry had landed at Maldon and sent a force to occupy the Roman River. There was some confusion between Roman Road and Roman Way and most of the Essex troops did not find the enemy. Another exercise involved an enemy force leaving Witham. The Essex Troop that was supposed to intercept them were surprised and captured because the enemy left Witham earlier than expected.

In 1913 the annual training camp was based in Colchester, and unfortunately the weather was not at its best. The mess tent was blown away by a powerful wind while the whole regiment was eating dinner.

The manoeuvres were based on a supposed war between Suffolk and Essex and seemed to have been more successful than the previous year. The Essex Force managed to stop three patrols from the Suffolk Force getting through the lines of men defending Colchester.

Regimental sports was a success, with events obviously aimed at being useful training aids, such as tent-pegging, mounted tug-of-war and horsemanship. There were Territorial Sunday parades in various areas aimed at enlisting new recruits. At Waltham Abbey the Essex Yeomanry paraded with the Herts Yeomanry. They were accompanied by the Dunmow town band and marched along Braintree Road through the town to the church. They paraded afterwards on the green opposite the clock house. There were also parades at Southend, Brentwood, Stratford and Grays.

Displays by the Yeomanry were quite common at various events in the county. Ingatestone Flower Show had a tent-pegging display, while on August bank holiday 1913 Danbury fête had displays of tent-pegging and races.

Once the war began, there were problems getting enough horses to supply the troops for the conflict. B. Todhunter was trying to obtain horses, but found that

A print showing the battle at Le Cateau on 26 August 1914. The 2nd Essex Regiment were part of the 3,000 members of the 12th Infantry Brigade who fought off an attack by 9,000 members of the German cavalry division.

Essex had been stripped of suitable mounts by August 1914. He had to travel as far as Suffolk to obtain more.

In May 1915 there were reports in the newspapers of a brilliant attack by the Essex Yeomanry on German trenches. The attack took place somewhere in northern France on 13 May. It was led by a Colonel Deacon, who was unfortunately reported missing after the attack. News arrived later that the colonel was in fact a German prisoner of war. The attack was undertaken by just over 300 men and resulted in 160 casualties.

A series of four photographs of the Zeppelin brought down over Essex on 23 September 1916. A few months before, Zeppelins had bombed Essex almost without any danger to themselves. However, by late 1916 a number of were brought down, mainly by pilots from Hornchurch.

FIVE

The Second World War to the Present Day

The outbreak of another war was to have the biggest effect on the county yet. Army camps reappeared, but this time the public were to play a major part in the conflict too. Numerous voluntary groups appeared, recruiting those who were too young or too old to join the forces. Air raid wardens, fire-fighters and, later, the Home Guard all added to the pressure on the population who were already working longer hours in industry to produce the goods needed to fight the

A number of the buildings from the war have been reused. This café on the coast at Mersea Island was built as a large gun emplacement.

The Second World War led to a new round of defensive buildings, including the best known and still most common; the pillbox. This one at Coalhouse Fort is unusual in having two storeys.

The ice-cream stand close to the café at Mersea Island was built as a searchlight base.

The Mustang was improved by the inclusion of a Rolls-Royce engine, as this advertisement by the company explains.

THE MUSTANG . . . .

"the longest-ranged single-engined fighter in the world."

The New York "Herald Tribune," commenting on the new Mustang, said: "Many have long regarded it as the best fighter plane produced in the States, but it remained for the British to discover it. If it had not been for British orders, it would never have-been developed at all. Its full potentialities were brought out only when the British designed Rolls-Royce Merlin engine was installed.

ROLLS-ROYCE

MERLIN ENGINES

war. As well as army camps, new air force bases sprang up across the county and men from all parts of the Commonwealth, and later from America, arrived to liven up the quiet towns and villages of Essex and give the county a more cosmopolitan feel. This was often a shock to small villages where the population rarely travelled far from their home and were not used to seeing visitors from other parts of the county, let alone other parts of the world.

BOREHAM AIRFIELD

Construction of the airfield began in May 1943 by the Americans, but was not occupied by US planes until March the following year. The first occupants of the airfield were the 394th Bomb Group. They flew B-26 Marauders and stayed until July 1944. Sadly, the construction led to the destruction of large areas of forest.

After some time as an emergency airfield, the 315th Troop Carrier Group of the United States Army Air Force were stationed at Boreham in March 1945. They carried the 6th British Airborne Division to drop by parachute during the crossing of the Rhine.

The airfield closed in 1945 and the huts on the field were used as temporary housing until the 1950s. There was also a racetrack on the site, which was used by the West Essex Car Club. It was then taken over by Ford Motor Company and used

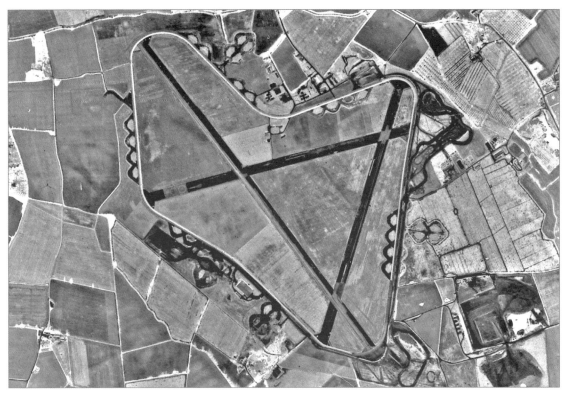

An aerial view of Boreham Airfield in the 1970s, showing the runways still in place.
(Ford Motor Company)

as a lorry-testing site, before again being used as a rally car racing site. In 1962 Ford spent a great deal of money on new buildings at the site.

The control tower is still on the old field, despite much of the area previously being used for gravel extraction. There are two large letters, 'J' and 'M', painted on the ground by the tower. These were the wartime identification letters for the airfield and allowed pilots to distinguish it from other airfields close by. It is now the base of the Essex Police Helicopter Unit and the Air Ambulance.

Pillboxes were mainly built on the coast, but were often in strategic positions inland. This one is next to the level crossing at Frinton station.

BOXTED AIRBASE

Boxted Airbase began construction in summer 1942 when it was given to the Eighth Air Force. It was eventually occupied and was used by a bombing group flying B-26s the following year commanded by Colonel Lester Maitland. Colonel Maitland, a well-known pilot, was supposedly the first man to fly at over 200mph.

Later the same year the airfield became a fighter base of the Ninth Air Force. They were the first to fly the P-51Bs. There were problems with the plane until the engines were changed to the Rolls-Royce Merlin. The 354th became known as the Pioneer Mustang Group and were commanded by Lieutenant Colonel Blakeslee who had previously served with the RAF Eagle Squadron.

The next group to arrive were the Wolfpack from Halesworth, Suffolk, flying P-47s with red painted cowlings. They were led by Colonel Hubert Zemke. There is a large stone memorial to Zemke's Wolfpack outside the air museum at Halesworth, Suffolk.

The 5th Emergency Rescue Group was formed in May 1944 and was also based at Boxted. They used P-47s, which were converted to carry dinghies instead of bombs, which they would drop to pilots who came down in the North Sea.

The RAF used the airfield for a few years after the war but it closed in 1947. Much of the old airfield has now been returned to farming.

Borough of Colchester

COLONEL G. L. CROSSMAN, C.M.G., D.S.O.
AIR RAID PRECAUTIONS OFFICER

TEL.: COLCHESTER 3458

VICTORIA CHAMBERS,
ST. RUNWALD STREET
COLCHESTER.

29 JUL 1938

Dear Sir (or Madam),

I have pleasure in sending you your Local Certificate of Anti-Gas Training and thank you on behalf of the Borough for your good work in taking the Course so successfully.

The silver Badge will be issued later in the Autumn when I am hoping to have them presented at a special Meeting.

Meanwhile I ask you to wait patiently until I have got far enough in the organisation to take you through practical demonstrations of actual First Aid Post work. As soon as possible, you will be notified as to the actual Post you will be allocated to.

Yours faithfully,

George Crossman.
Colonel,
Air-Raid Precautions Officer.

Preparations for air raids – including the use of gas – were well underway before the outbreak of war, as this letter shows.

BRADWELL

Bradwell Bay airfield was one of the lesser-known airbases of the war. This was due to its connection with radar, which was such a well-kept secret early in the war that many of the pilots themselves were unaware of its existence. The field was built in 1941 on the banks of the Blackwater, near Bradwell-juxta-Mare. There had in fact been a landing site there before the war for planes using a practice firing range on Dengie Flats. The Germans must have had an idea of the planned airfield, as the site was actually bombed before the airfield was built. From April 1942, Canadian Squadron 418 flew Douglas Boston bombers from the base.

Later the same year, the 23rd Squadron, RAF, arrived with de Havilland Mosquitoes. A number of other RAF squadrons spent time at the base before the 488 New Zealand Squadron arrived.

Many of the men from the airfield were billeted in the village at Down Hall and Bradwell Lodge. In 1944, just before D-Day, they were moved out of the houses into tents – to toughen up in preparation for the invasion.

The airfield had an innovative system for dispersing fog. It was known as FIDO: Fog Investigation Dispersal Operation. It worked by burning pipes full of petrol, which ran alongside the runway. The heat then dispersed the fog.

Czech fighter pilots came to the airfield early in 1945 to help deal with the menace of V-1s. The field closed in August 1945.

CLACTON

The Second World War put a stop to the development of Clacton as a seaside town. Although many evacuees must have thought themselves lucky to have been sent to the seaside at the beginning of the war, it quickly became evident that far from being a safe haven the town's children were themselves in need of evacuation. Its newly arrived evacuees and Clacton's own children were quickly packed off to safer places.

Clacton had the notorious distinction of being the site of the first civilian casualties of the war, when a German plane crashed on a house in the town in early 1940. Along with other seaside towns, defences were erected along the beaches, and at nearby Holland-on-Sea a large fort was erected on the cliff tops. Once again the Napoleonic Martello towers came back into use as defensive structures.

COLCHESTER

Colchester was another town thought to be safe enough to take evacuees from London early in the war – although how anyone could believe that a garrison town would be safe for evacuated children is a mystery. There was soon a dramatic change in policy and not only were the evacuees moved but so were the children of Colchester themselves.

This policy was the correct thing to do as Colchester suffered air raids throughout the war, although fatalities were not as heavy as they could have been with just over fifty people killed. Nearly forty of these were killed in one raid when bombs fell on

The 2nd Battalion, the Royal Fusiliers, at Colchester in 1930. Obviously a very successful unit in army sports as shown by the trophies.

After the war, the Eighth Air Force of the United States Army presented the Borough of Colchester with a seventeenth-century silver rose bowl (above) in thanks of their treatment by locals. The bowl is still part of the Borough Regalia.

The mayor of the time, local dignitaries and members of the US Army Air force in the Town Hall.
Castle

Severalls Mental Hospital. There were of course many more injuries, and damage to several of the factories in the town affected output of much needed war materials.

One factory directly involved in wartime production was Paxman's. The workforce numbered more than 2,000 during the war and they produced engines for several types of wartime vehicles. Other factories produced uniforms and even parachute material.

There were of course thousands of soldiers from around the world, as well as from all parts of Britain, based in the town. Alongside regular troops billeted in the town were girls from the Women's Land Army and those who chose to work in industry rather than on the land. All the newcomers had to be found somewhere to stay; some lived in hostels.

On 10 July 1945, a special meeting of the council was convened at the Town Hall, which included the mayor Alderman Piper. The meeting was called to express the thanks of the council to representatives of the 55th and 355th Fighter Groups and the 440th and 442nd Air Service Groups of the United States Army. The Americans presented a seventeenth-century silver rose bowl for inclusion among the

The mayor and local dignitaries and the members of the US Army Air Force in the castle.
town hall

Corporation Regalia of the Colchester Council. This was in thanks for the friendly welcome that the people of Colchester and the surrounding areas had shown to the American Forces. The event was captured by an official photographer from one of the American bases.

DAGENHAM

By the outbreak of the Second World War, Dagenham had grown from a small village into one of the largest council estates in the world. Built by the Greater London Council, the homes were built to re-house the families from the disappearing slums of the City of London.

Much of the war work was carried out in the dock area of the town on the banks of the Thames. The three tugs belonging to the Samuel Williams Co. at the dock were sent immediately when the appeal went out for small craft to help out with the evacuation of Dunkirk. The tugs were named *Prince*, *Princess* and *Duke*. The *Prince* and *Princess* towed the Isle of Wight ferry across to the French coast, only to be turned back within a few miles of the shore. The *Duke* reached the shore and took

Although ignored as a source of war materials at first, the photograph shows how important Ford became to the war effort later in the war. *(Ford Motor Co.)*

some men aboard and later took on men from the lifeboat of a sunken ship. After being signalled by a plane, the tug then found two more lifeboats and picked up the survivors.

Another company based at Dagenham was the Hudson Steamship Co., whose ships carried coal from the north of England to London. They lost a number of their ships to enemy action; many of these had local names such as the *Upminster*, the *Hornchurch*, and the *Dagenham*, which, although damaged, was not sunk. The *Dagenham* went on to play a part in the D-Day landings – making several trips to rescue soldiers from the Normandy beaches.

What would seem to have been one of the most useful factories for producing goods for the war effort was also found on the banks of the Thames at Dagenham. Its location, however, was one reason that the government refused to grant it any contracts early in the war. The Ford Motor factory was in too exposed a position, which made it an ideal target for German bombers. This proved to be the case as nearly 200 bombs fell on the factory during the war, but even this did not manage to hold up production for any length of time.

The arrival of Churchill as Prime Minister changed the government's attitude towards the company, and by the middle of 1940 Ford was working on several government contracts. Not only were they producing vehicles for the war effort but the slag from the blast furnace made ideal material for use in building airfield runways.

As well as providing the country with vehicles and aircraft engines, Ford had its own Home Guard unit numbering around 600 men. Their first weapons were 8ft-long pikes, which they received at the end of 1941. During one exercise the factory was attacked by regular army units. It began at midnight and the factory Home Guard unit held out until the early hours of the morning when the Royal Norfolk Regiment finally captured part of the factory.

DEBDEN AIRFIELD

Debden was opened before the Second World War, in April 1937, but work was carried out on extending it well into the war years. There were several different aircraft flying from the field in the early years of the war. The main early planes at the field were Hurricanes. Members of the Royal Canadian Air Force were also based at Debden in 1941, before moving to Bradwell the following year.

There was a strange incident at the airfield in February 1941 when a plane that had been circling the field finally landed. The pilot got out of the plane and went to speak to the men manning the control tower. The pilot was German. The plane was a Heinkel 111, which quickly took off again. There were a number of similar cases where German planes had become lost and landed at English airfields, especially at night, thinking that they were in France.

In May 1943, Debden became an American airbase. This involved the transfer of the RAF Eagle Squadrons manned by American volunteers to the American Air Force. The Eagle Squadrons had been at Debden and were part of the RAF but consisted of Americans who volunteered to fight before their country entered the war. They continued to fly Spitfires for some time after their transfer until changing to P-47s.

Debden Airfield was taken over by the army in 1975. One old hangar and a radar station still remain there. There is also a memorial at the site.

EARLS COLNE AIRFIELD

The construction of Earls Colne Airfield began in 1941 as part of a large airfield building project in East Anglia. It was given to the RAF on completion in 1942 but was not put to much use until the following year. When the United States Army Air Force's 94th Bomb Group arrived at the base in May 1943, it was one of the first airfields in the country to have the famous Flying Fortress based there. These planes were bigger than any aircraft most people had ever seen, and were manned by a crew of ten.

The planes only stayed a few weeks however before moving to Rougham in Suffolk. On the day they moved nine of the planes were shot down over the

The Flying Fortress must have amazed locals with its size. The planes were common over Essex once the Americans arrived and Britain became America's 'unsinkable aircraft carrier'. *(N. Challoner)*

North Sea. They left Earls Colne for their mission, but on their return to Rougham were attacked by Junkers 88s. The crews had supposedly begun to strip and clean their guns before the attack, which was not supposed to happen until they had landed.

The Fortresses were replaced at the airfield by the 323rd Bomb Group flying B-26 Marauders. These became common planes in the county when Marauders were based at a number of other Essex airfields. The bomber groups in the area were controlled from an ancient mansion close to Earls Colne Airfield. Marks Hall was the headquarters of the ninth US Army Air Force bomber command.

After taking part in D-Day, the Marauders from Earls Colne and other Essex bases moved to airfields on the continent. Earls Colne was taken over by the RAF, from where Albemarles and Halifaxes flew drop parachutists in Europe. This involved agents working for the Special Operations Executive who joined with resistance groups in occupied countries.

FAIRLOP AIRFIELD

Fairlop was originally a First World War airfield called Hainault, but was closed at the end of the war and returned to use as farmland. This was not the first use of the area by aviators. When Handley Page set up an aircraft factory at Barking Creek in 1911 the site was found to be unsuitable as an airfield, so a sports field at Fairlop was used as an aerodrome for the factory. There were plans to develop the area as a civilian airfield in the late 1930s but due to the threat of war it was decided a fighter base would be more useful and it was rebuilt in 1941 as RAF Fairlop. The airfield was unusual in that it had three concrete runways; many of the early fields were still grass. There was also enough accommodation for over 1,000 men. The first planes on the field were Spitfires

The Spitfire was probably the most successful fighter plane of the Battle of Britain.

One of the old hangars from Fairlop being used as a playschool in 2000. *(N. Challoner)*

of 603 Squadron. There was also a Czechoslovakian Squadron based at the field along with numerous others.

In 1943 the Spitfires were replaced with Typhoons, which were used as bombers as well as fighters. They could also carry rockets fitted under their wings. The field was placed on a care and maintenance footing in early 1944.

The airfield later became a balloon site, which was largely manned by WAAFs. Before this, one of the main balloon sites in the area had been at RAF Chigwell, which was close to Fairlop. By the time the balloons arrived at Fairlop, however, they were already being run down at Chigwell so their life at Fairlop did not last long.

The site of the airfield is now mainly covered by Hainault Forest Country Park and little that remains of the old site.

FOULNESS

Although Foulness was originally part of the Shoeburyness firing ranges, only part is currently left and stands alone as a weapons testing area. Although the testing ranges in the area have had a generally friendly relationship with its neighbours during its history, this may not be true of the site now.

Foulness has become a restricted area to everyone except its inhabitants and is now run by a private agency named QinetiQ on behalf of the government. Despite the apparent secrecy in the recent past, delegations from various local councils have been allowed to visit the site due to complaints. Although mainly from Essex, some were from Kent.

The main objection made by locals seems to be that not only are the sand flats used for recovery of weapons fired, but that the site is also used to destroy out of date munitions.

At St Osyth, equipment was installed to monitor explosions at the site. There have been complaints in the area of damage to the walls of buildings and to items inside them due to the explosions.

GOSFIELD

Gosfield was the site of a strange event in 1940 when a soldier vanished without trace. One explanation was that the soldier, driver James Meecham RASC, a survivor of Dunkirk, was keeping crowds back from a crater after an air raid when the ground collapsed, burying him alive. According to Meecham's sister, James was on guard duty near the site of an exploded bomb when a policeman turned to speak to him – only to find that he had disappeared. His sister believes that another bomb had exploded underground, which led to his being swallowed by the earth. Despite three days of digging by soldiers his body was never found.

AIR RAID PRECAUTIONS
HANDBOOK No. 2
(3rd Edition)

FIRST AID AND NURSING FOR GAS CASUALTIES

LONDON
HIS MAJESTY'S STATIONERY OFFICE
Price 4*d.* net

One of many booklets produced by the government before and during the war giving instructions on what to do during air raids.

HARWICH

Harwich had a history of suffering economic decline after conflict. It had happened after the French wars of the nineteenth century and it happened again at the end of the First World War. Although all parts of the country suffered during the depression, Harwich was particularly badly affected. There was a shift of population towards Dovercourt, and as a result Harwich became more deserted.

The headquarters of the Essex and Suffolk Royal Garrison Artillery, who operated the guns at Beacon Hill. The building is currently used as offices.

By the time the Second World War began, much of the old War Department property in Harwich had been sold to the local council. As members of the public left the town due to the danger, the empty houses they left behind were used as billets for the influx of servicemen to the town. One of the first major casualties of the war was the destroyer HMS *Gypsy*, which was hit by a mine and sank just off the Harwich coast. Locals remember the explosion shaking the whole town.

The Harwich Redoubt, which had been built to defend against invasion by Napoleon, had been acquired by the local council in the 1930s. Houses were built around it and the Redoubt fell into disrepair, this was aided by the council stripping out many of its interior effects such as the floorboards. During the war it came back into military control and was used as a prison.

After the war it was again left to deteriorate, and by the late 1960s the council were prepared to sell the land to property developers. The resulting publicity brought the presence of the Redoubt to the notice of many locals who knew little about it, and it was then that the Harwich Society began its process of restoring the defence which included retrieving an enormous cannon, which had been buried, from the moat.

The higher towers at Beacon Hill were in use in the Second World War, when having less visible defences was no longer so important.

HORNCHURCH

The airbase at Hornchurch had an effect on the local population in many ways. It was obviously dangerous to live near the base because of the threat of air attacks. There were more positive effects however. Anne Whitehead (née Vines) lived in Hornchurch and owing to the war only attended school in the mornings. Children would spend the time after air raids collecting shrapnel.

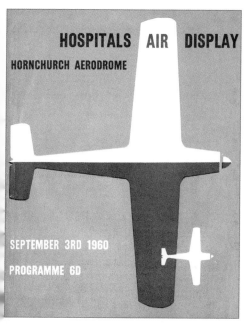

RAF Hornchurch was in existence until the 1960s and often held air displays in aid of charity, as this programme shows. The display included a Spitfire.

Below: The memorial to RAF Hornchurch in the grounds of R.J. Mitchell School.

The Good Intent pub sign showing a Spitfire. The pub is on the site of the old airbase.

Below: The cemetery at St Andrew's Church in Hornchurch contains military graves from both world wars. They includes the graves of several Maoris who were based in the town with New Zealand Forces during the First World War. The photograph shows the section devoted to men from the Second World War.

Anne attended St Mary's Roman Catholic School and remembers a Christmas party for Catholic children organised by Polish airmen from RAF Hornchurch. She also remembers queuing for chocolate powder at an American base situated in Upper Rainham Road, where the old council depot used to be. The site is now a new housing estate.

LITTLE CHESTERFORD

Springwell House in Little Chesterford may not have played much part in the war but one of its inhabitants of over thirty years did. Admiral Sir Gilbert Stephenson was already in his sixties when the Second World War broke out, but this did not stop him from being present on the beaches during the evacuation from Dunkirk.

It was after this however that he was given his best known posting – as the Commander of the Special Training School set up as part of the Western Approaches Command in the small fishing town of Tobermory on the island of Mull. It was a real-life job that was fictionalised in the famous book *The Cruel Sea* by Nicholas Monsarrat.

The admiral's task was to undertake short training courses for the new crew members aboard corvettes, frigates, sloops and Patrol Service trawlers. Many of the crew were members of the Naval Reserve and were ex-fishermen who displayed little of the discipline of the average naval recruit.

Many Navy personnel looked down upon them, but at the time they played a vital role in defending the country and did an amazing job clearing mines and even fighting U-boats. One of the men under the admiral's command was the newsreader Richard Baker, who later wrote a book about him entitled *The Terror of Tobermory*.

After retirement there was little change in the direct action of the admiral. He was taken to court for keeping a loaded gun by his bed. His argument in court was that there was no point in keeping an unloaded gun by the bed, for would an intruder wait while he loaded it?

POINT CLEAR

Point Clear was the site of one of the first Essex Martello towers, which stretched eastwards along the coast during the Napoleonic Wars. As in other conflicts, the towers were brought back into use as defensive structures during the Second World War. The Point Clear tower was subjected to a number of modifications for the needs of modern warfare: an observation window was installed to give a view across the Colne and Blackwater Estuaries to nearby Brightlingsea and further across to Mersea Island and as far as Bradwell, while on the roof new structures were added as well as new, more modern guns.

The Point Clear tower was for some time the only Martello in Essex open to the public, although the one at Jaywick has now been opened as an arts centre. Point Clear tower is currently the home of the East Essex Aviation Society and Museum. It has a fine collection of weapons and uniforms of the Second World War. It also has a number of remains of aircraft that crashed in the local area during the war.

The Martello tower at Point Clear was used during the Second World War. It is now a museum.

The view from the top of the tower, looking over the estuaries of the River Colne and the Blackwater. The tower was used as a lookout point during the war.

PURFLEET

Between the wars the use of Purfleet ranges was relaxed somewhat and they became a shortcut for people walking to the rubbish tips by the Thames. The matter of trespass was overlooked for most of the year but one day a year a man was posted on the shortcut to warn those using it that it was still government property.

The ranges were also used for shooting by local members of the Rainham Rifle Club. They used to meet in the Phoenix pub on a Sunday morning. The licences of club members were regularly checked by the local police.

The ranges were still used by the army between the wars. Many of the soldiers practising on the ranges would visit the canteens of factories in Ferry Lane to get a cup of tea.

One of the remaining buildings from Purfleet Barracks. This was once used as a chapel.

There were several bases for war workers in the area around Purfleet. Wennington Hall Farm had an auxiliary fire service, which used cars with ladders on the roof and trailers with pumps for fire fighting. Prisoners of war also worked on local farms, as there were a number of camps in the area. One camp in Fen Lane, Orsett, was used by the army, then as a PoW camp before becoming a base for Land Girls. Prisoners of war were also based at Wennington House.

RIVENHALL AIRBASE

Rivenhall Airbase was in fact closer to the village of Silver End than Rivenhall and was known locally as Silver Hall Aerodrome. It was built in 1943 with one company laying the runways while another constructed the buildings.

The first units at the field were an American fighter group; the 363rd. They were waiting for new planes when they first arrived. They were also short of pilots. Some pilots were transferred from Suffolk, where there were more American bases than there were in Essex.

The final American operation from Rivenhall took place in August 1944, and the airfield was then handed over to the RAF. It was to be a few months before Stirling bombers arrived. There were also gliders at the base, which were to be used for more attacks on Europe. The airfield also had involvement with the Special Operations Executive, which was responsible for dropping supplies and agents to resistance groups in the occupied countries of Europe.

After its closure as an airfield, the site went through a number of uses common to post-war airfields and army camps. It became the home of released Polish prisoners of war for a time, then became a sort of casual ward for tramps, and was later taken over by the Marconi Company for use in radar experiments.

SOUTHEND

Southend Airport reopened in 1935 after closing at the end of the First World War. The RAF Volunteer Reserve and the Civil Air Guard were based there in 1936. They were joined in 1937 by the Auxiliary Squadrons of 602 City of Glasgow and 607 County of Durham. By 1939 the part-timers had become full-time and were flying Spitfires.

One of the first squadrons to be based at the field was 54 Squadron, who flew Spitfires there from 1939. However, it wasn't until early 1940 that they finally saw action. Number 74 squadron were also based at the airfield and saw action earlier. They were responsible for shooting down the first German plane brought down over England; a Heinkel 111 over the Thames in November 1939. Mr T. Farmer, who lived in the area as a child, remembers hearing the fighter planes at the airfield warming up their engines in the mornings.

The airfield was small, with only two old hangars and a clubhouse. There were no proper barracks for the men based there. The railway line ran along its eastern edge, which made landing difficult. The pilots who used the airfield early in the war came from Hornchurch where the facilities were much better.

COUNTY BOROUGH OF SOUTHEND-ON-SEA.

BOROUGH ENGINEER'S DEPARTMENT.

AIR RAID PRECAUTIONS.

A N D E R S O N   S H E L T E R S.

(Advice to the Public on Proper
Protection).

- -

Anderson Shelters are designed to afford to the
occupants the standard degree of protection against blast and
splinter and debris.

They will only do this if the following precautions
are taken:-

1. The shelter should be surrounded on top and at the
   sides and back and at the sides of the front
   entrance by earth. The thickness of the earth
   must not be less than 15 inches over the arched
   portion of the shelter, and 30 inches at the sides,
   front and back. The earth should be well
   consolidated.

   The thickness of 30 inches at the sides is best
   obtained by sloping the earth down to ground level,
   but if there is not room for this, it may be
   supported by a small wall of bricks, concrete, etc.

2. The entrance should be protected. If it is within
   15 feet of a brick or other substantial building,
   no further protection is needed. If it is more
   than 15 feet from a building, a small blast wall of
   earth, sandbags, brickwork, or something of the same
   sort should be constructed in front of the entrance
   to screen the inside of the shelter from the direct
   effect of blast.

3. The emergency exit at the back should be capable
   of being worked. The method of opening the
   emergency exit is to turn down the two clips which
   hold in the upper portion of the middle sheet, and
   to pull inwards into the shelter the middle sheet.
   Any earth outside can be then removed from inside
   the shelter, provided there is a suitable tool kept
   in the shelter.

   The proper maintenance of shelters which have been
supplied free to householders is the responsibility of the
householders and not of the Corporation. This includes seeing
to the provision of the proper thicknesses of earth, blast wall
if necessary, etc.

Instructions on how to erect an Anderson Shelter, issued by the Southend Borough Engineers'
Department.

P A R A H U T E M I N E S. (L.A. 228 & 234 and
O. & T.M. 18).

ᵣe.   Do not use other descriptions, such as "Land Mines,"
"Parachute Bombs', etc.

entification.(L.A. 234 and 235).
The diagrams below may help to identify a parachute mine.
The ᵣarachute is frequently found at a distance from the
actual mine.

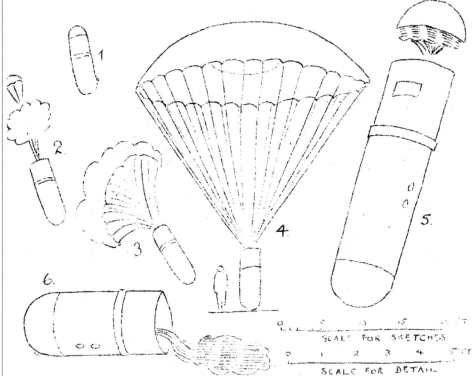

SCALE FOR SKETCHES

SCALE FOR DETAIL

Mine as it leaves 'plane Parachute is folded inside top.
'Top, pulling parachute out of 4 manilla cords; parachute is attached
by its own silk cords on a ring to a shackle-bolt inside mine.
Parachute opening out; cap now freed by rip cord.
Mine in descent (note circular spillway in top of parachute).
6'0" man is shown to same scale to give size.
5. Detail of mine with cap,A, just free (parachute is inside cap).
Explosive (Hexanite) is in the bottom portion,C, with its two fuses,
magnetic and **vibration** and detonator. Tail portion,B, containing
magnetic mechanism is bolted with $\frac{7}{8}$" hexagonal brass nuts to base
'C' and should on no account be removed, even if nearly broken off,
nor should inspection door in centre be touched.
ᴼTE. There are two sizes of Mines, approximately 8'0" and 5'0" long
respectively. (see 6).

It appears, from experience, that Parachute Mines are usually
dropped from enemy aircraft in pairs; when only one mine is
located a search should be made for a second, which may land
several miles away from the first. It should not be assumed that

Instructions for air raid wardens in Southend on how to recognise parachute mines.

Shoeburyness Barracks near Southend is now a private housing estate. Chapel Place has an old cannon in the centre and the chapel is now the sales office for the estate.

In 1940 the airfield became RAF Southend, and several houses were requisitioned as billets for the men. Until then they had slept in the clubhouse. The airfield also took over the golf club where the clubhouse became a sergeants' mess.

The field reopened on a commercial basis in 1946. Apart from use as an airport, Southend has been the site of an annual air show since 1986. Unlike other air shows that take place on the airfields themselves, Southend's main flying display site is the seafront.

The town itself was well fortified in case of invasion. Mr T. Farmer lived at Kent Elms Corner as a child and remembered there being anti-tank blocks on each side of the road and pillboxes on the corners. Because Southend was a restricted area during invasion scares, soldiers or policemen would check identity cards on the buses going to Southend.

There were large military convoys moving around the town, which included tanks. At night there was the noisy sound of the anti-aircraft guns at Belfairs Park. One of Mr Farmer's teachers was killed by a V-2 on Christmas Eve. It landed in his back garden in the Eastwood area of the town.

The old clock tower at Shoeburyness is still in place and is the entrance to a green surrounded by private houses.

STANSTED

Construction began on the airfield at Stansted in the summer of 1942 making it one of the first American bases to be built in the area. It was built by the Americans themselves, and was opened as a USAAF base in August 1943.

After some time as a service depot, a bomb group arrived in early 1944 and flew B-26 aircraft. The planes were left unpainted and became known as the Silver Streaks.

In 1945, Stansted became a storage base and later a rest area for aircrews returning from Europe. After being handed over to the RAF, Stansted became a PoW camp.

The Hurricane was another successful fighter plane during the Battle of Britain, as this wartime advertisement shows.

The origins of commercial flight began in 1946 when a company used old Halifax bombers as cargo planes. The Americans returned in the mid-1950s and the base was extended for use by jet aircraft. When the Americans left again in the late 1950s the airfield was put to a number of different uses mostly concerned with flying.

In December 1980, an American Air Force plane was diverted to Stansted due to weather problems at Mildenhall. Larry Warren described the arrival of Stansted in his book *Left at East Gate* as an inactive airport north of London. A man named Charles, dressed in a British Airways uniform, greeted them and told the new arrivals of plans to expand the airport to rival Heathrow and Gatwick. It was in fact a number of years before the decision was finally made to turn Stansted into London's third airport.

WALTHAM ABBEY

Although Waltham Abbey was used mainly as a research site before the war it was still producing huge quantities of cordite during the Second World War, but much of the production was later moved to the West Country, further away from the bombing. Staff from the site were responsible for helping to set up new factories, so their work led to the end of the Waltham Abbey site, which shut down in 1943.

Waltham Abbey reopened in 1945 as a research centre investigating new forms of explosives for weapons, such as rocket-related items. The centre then lasted until 1991 when it again closed. It is currently open to the public.

WALTON-ON-THE-NAZE

The Naze in Walton was taken over by the military as part of Essex coastal defences. It was manned by various units from a number of different regiments who rotated their duties on coastal defence duties. Many of these men were from Scottish regiments, as had many of those stationed at Weeley during the nineteenth century. The orders for the defending troops were to fight to the last man and not to retreat in the event of an invasion.

The defences erected on the coast included pillboxes every few hundred yards along the beach plus some on the cliff top. These were mainly disguised as beach huts and other seaside amenities. Barbed wire and minefields also lined the beaches. These mines were often set off by movement in the cliffs, which have been receding for a number of years. A number of the pillboxes still survive.

Similar defences were erected around the coast in Frinton, Holland and Clacton. There were also two sea forts positioned off the coast of Walton. They were named Rough Tower and Sunk Head and were armed with two 3.7 anti-aircraft guns and two Bofors guns. Roughs can still be seen from the Naze.

The Roughs tower has had an interesting life since the war. Abandoned by the forces, it was used by pirate radio stations for a time until a former army major named Bates took the fort over in the 1960s. Bates declared it independent and actually fired a shot across the bows of a Trinity House ship that approached it. He was arrested while on a visit to the mainland, but the court found that the fort was outside British jurisdiction.

The Martello tower at Walton. It is now surrounded by the Martello caravan site.

The beach at the Naze is still lined with pillboxes.

The cliffs at the Naze were lined with guns during the war. These are now gone but there are still a few pillboxes in existence on the cliff top.

Known as Sealand, with its own stamps and passports, the fort was taken over by a group of Dutch men and one German in 1978. Bates went back and threw the men off, holding the German – who held a Sealand passport – as a prisoner of war. Sealand was put up for sale in 2007 as the world's smallest country.

The Naze tower came under threat during the war from a high-ranking army officer, who wanted it demolished because it was such a visible landmark for enemy attack. It later became a radar station.

One interesting event that occurred early in the war in the area was when the Japanese steamer *Terukuni Maru* was sunk by their future allies the Germans while on its way to London.

The local population were given leaflets by the government informing them that it may be necessary to evacuate the area in the event of invasion. This conflicted with other instructions to stay put in the event of invasion. This latter was stated more forcefully on later leaflets. The reasons for this were given that fleeing refugees could block the roads stopping British forces reaching the invasion area. Refugees could also be used as a shield by the enemy or even attacked to cause panic. The public were also warned not to become involved in battles.

The area of Walton was so important to the defence of the country that it was visited by Winston Churchill early in the war and later by Montgomery, who came to inspect the invasion forces based there. Following D-Day, the country faced a new onslaught in the shape of flying bombs. The Naze, with its large number of anti-aircraft guns positioned along the cliffs, became an important site in bringing down these weapons.

The RAF memorial in Walton churchyard, with the propellers from a Canadian aircraft brought down during the war.

WARLEY

The 1st Battalion of the Essex Regiment spent much of the inter-war years at Colchester and Pembroke Dock before being sent to France a few years before the war. The 2nd Battalion had been abroad. They had spent seventeen years in Turkey and India before arriving back at Warley in 1937. The spell in India was a connection with the former residents of Warley Barracks, the East India Company.

A First World War memorial in the Garrison Chapel at Warley.

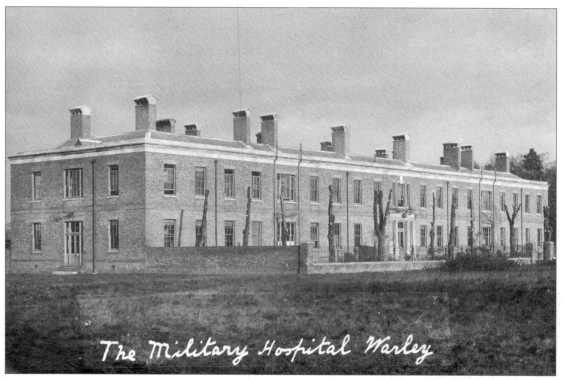

The hospital at Warley Barracks has long since gone, along with most of the other buildings.

The arrival of the 2nd Battalion at Warley was similar to that of many of the regiments that stayed at Warley in that a band played as they marched to the barracks from Brentwood station. They left Warley again to take part in the Coronation of George VI, and shortly afterwards again left the barracks for a spell in the Tower of London – not a new posting for the Essex Regiment, but an honour nevertheless.

Many of the men from the 2nd Battalion were transferred to the 1st Battalion in the years before the war. It was not until 1939 that the influx of new recruits began to arrive at Warley and the 2nd Battalion was returned to full strength. In the period before the war, the 1st Battalion was stationed in Egypt and had been on alert since the Italian invasion of Abyssinia in April 1939. One of their tasks was to guard against a ship being scuttled and blocking the Suez Canal.

Many of the territorial units called up were used to reinforce the regular army. One of these was the 4th Battalion of the Essex Regiment, which had been called up in 1939 and was used to reinforce the 1st Battalion in Egypt. After fighting in many parts of the Middle East, the battalion moved to India before returning to England in 1944 where they were quartered at Roman Way Camp in Colchester.

When the war seemed inevitable, the 2nd Battalion were at Warley. The main worry about the outbreak of hostilities was that air raids would begin immediately.

The officers' mess, which has since been converted into a private care home.

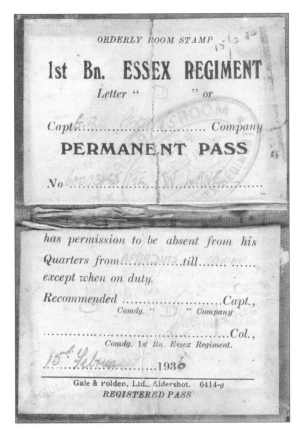

A pass for a member of the 1st Battalion of the Essex Regiment, dating from 1930.

Men from Essex served all over the world during the war. This is B Company of 1/4th Essex Regiment at Monte Cassino.

The 2nd Battalion was therefore sent to defend London under the direction of Anti-Aircraft Command. Small units were sent all over the capital armed with Lewis and Bren guns.

When war did come, the 2nd Battalion returned to Warley. They were soon on their way to Brest. They were later moved to Lille where they were responsible for building defences. It was some time later that the attack came from the Germans, and the 2nd Essex had the dubious honour of being the first unit to be dive-bombed. The battalion was forced to fight its way back to Dunkirk. There they were picked up by the destroyer *Whitehall* and landed at Dover. The next four years were spent at various camps either training or on coastal guard duty until 1944 when they went back to France on D-Day.

Several other units of the Essex Regiment played a part in the war both at home and abroad. In August 1939 the Territorial Army was put on readiness, and the headquarters of the 1/4th Battalion was at Ilford. There were also companies at Dagenham, Burnham, Manor Park and Epping. The battalion was then ordered to billets at Epping. They later moved to Witham before being split between Maldon, North Weald and Hornchurch on defensive duties. They were later sent to the north of England before being shipped to West Africa in 1940.

The 2/4th Battalion were formed at Ilford at the same time as the 1/4th. They started out in a similar vein guarding important sites mainly at Clacton, Dagenham, Shoeburyness and Romford. They were later sent to Suffolk on coastal guard duty. Later they also went to the north of England. They spent the war moving around the country in the role of coastal defence troops and also taking part in several training exercises.

Colonel Noble leads the 1/4th battalion of the Essex Regiment in Tripoli, 1943.

The *Eagle* journal of the Essex Regiment from 1946.

Not all Essex men were based in Essex. John Smith from Romford was in the Far East fighting the Japanese with the RAF Regiment. News from home was rare, so English papers were eagerly read. John is at the back on the right. *(John Smith)*

At the beginning of the war the 1/5th Essex Battalion was based at Chelmsford. They also spent the early part of the war in coastal defence and training. The battalion was soon moved to the north of England. There were plans to send them overseas in August 1940 but this was cancelled. They later moved to Kent for coastal defence duties before being sent to the Middle East in 1941.

In 1948 the 1st Battalion took over the East Anglian Brigade Training Centre and was later amalgamated with the 2nd Battalion. This ceremony took place at Meanee Barracks in Colchester on 3 November 1948.

Bibliography

BOOKS

Astbury, A., *Estuary*, Carnforth Press, 1980

Banks, T.M. & Chell, R.A., *With the 10th Essex in France*, Burt & Sons, 1921

Barfoot, J., *Essex Airmen: 1910–1918*, Tempus, 2006

Barret ,C.R.B., *Essex Highways, Byways and Waterways*, Lawrence & Bullen, 1892

Blackwell, E. & Axe, E., *Romford to Beirut*, R.W. Humphries, 1926

Bundock, J., *Old Leigh*, Phillimore, 1978

Carter, M., 'The Fort of Othona and the Chapel of St Peter on the Wall, Bradwell', Provost and Chapter of Chelmsford, 1967

Clark, A., *Excavations at Mucking*, English Heritage, 1993

Hallmann, R., *Essex: History You Can See*, Tempus, 2006

Hibberd, D., *Wilfred Owen*, Weidenfeld & Nicolson, 2002

Martin, G., *The Story of Colchester*, Benham Newspapers Ltd, 1959

Pollitt, W., *The Rise of Southend*, John H. Burrows & Sons, 1957

Pyke, C., *Rainham and Wennington*, Tempus, 2005

Smith, G., *Smuggling in Essex*, Countryside Books, 2005

Starley, D., 'Assessment of metalworking debris from Uphall Camp', English Heritage, 1997

Warren, L. & Robbins, P., *Left at East Gate*, Marlowe & Company, 1997

NEWSPAPERS, JOURNALS & PERIODICALS

Daily Mirror, 23 February 1915

East Anglian Archaeology, Bond, D., 'Excavations at the North Ring, Mucking, Essex', 1988

Essex Archaeological Transactions, Crouch, W., 'Uphall Camp', Vol. 9, 1906

Essex Archaeology & History, 19, Powell, W., 'Medieval Hospitals at East and West Tilbury and Henry VIII's Blockhouses', 1988

Essex Countryside, Cooper, W., 'The Saga of Harwich Redoubt', November 1971

——, Haines, L., 'The Neglected Mersea Island Barrow', June 1967

——, Harper, G., 'Essex Knights in the Civil War', May 1967

——, Korbacz, E., 'Mersea's Forgotten Fort', May 1971

——, Priestley, H., 'An Essex-Born Soldier of Fortune', November 1971

——, Wilson, S., 'When I Joined the Essex Territorial', July 1973

——, [unknown author] 'The Soldier Who Disappeared in Essex', September 1969

——, [unknown author] 'The Southend Zeppelin Raid', August 1969
Essex Review, 'Benham & Co.', April 1926
——, 'Benham & Co.', July 1926
——, 'Record of Mark Crummie', vol. 55
Essex Review, Pressey, Revd W., 'Echoes of the Spanish Armada', 1926
Essex Times, 19 September 1914; 7 November 1914; 28 November 1914; 19
    December 1914; 26 June 1915; 23 July 1915
Illustrated London News, 'The Transvaal War', 1900
Journal of the British Archaeological Association, Burrows, J., 'Tilbury Fort', 1932
London Archaeologist, Greenwood P., 'Uphall Camp, An Iron Age Fortification',
    Autumn 1989
——, Greenwood P., 'Uphall Camp, An Iron Age Fortification', Spring 2001
Romford Times, 20 January 1915; 5 February 1915; 26 May 1915; 1 September
    1915
The Railway Magazine, 'Sequestrator, Shoeburyness Military Tramway', April 1959
Transactions of the Essex Field Club, Vol. 1, Walker, H. 'A Day's Elephant Hunting
    in Essex', 1880

ESSEX RECORD OFFICE DOCUMENTS

An Act for the Preservation and Improvement of Harwich Harbour, 28 July 1863
An Act for Compensation to Proprietors of Lands for the Use of His Majesty's
Ordnance at Warley Common, 21 July 1806
Circular from the Archbishop of Canterbury, D/P 200/1/33
Crime Report, Barrack Dept D/DEL L/4
Defence of Essex Report, T/A 218/1
Imperial War Museum, Ferrie Captain W.S., 03/19/1
Letters to the Poor Law Commission, D/P 66/19/2
Mildmay Letters D/Dmy/15M50/84/1
Military Memoir T/A 218/1
Royal Commission on Historical Monuments, Essex South East, HMSO, 1923
Royal Commission on Historical Monuments, Essex North East, HMSO, 1922

Index